W9-CAU-674

Man Equals Man

and

The Elephant Calf

Works of Bertolt Brecht
published by
Arcade

Baal

The Caucasian Chalk Circle

Collected Stories

The Good Person of Szechwan

The Good Person of Szechwan, Mother Courage and Her Children, and *Fear and Misery of the Third Reich*

Life of Galileo

Life of Galileo, The Resistible Rise of Arturo Ui, and *The Caucasian Chalk Circle*

Man Equals Man and *The Elephant Calf*

Mother Courage and Her Children

Mother Courage and Her Children, adapted by David Hare

Mr. Puntila and His Man Matti

The Rise and Fall of the City of Mahagonny and *The Seven Deadly Sins of the Petty Bourgeoisie*

Saint Joan of the Stockyards

Schweyk and the Second World War and *The Visions of Simone Machard*

The Threepenny Opera

The Threepenny Opera, Baal, and *The Mother*

BERTOLT BRECHT

Man Equals Man

and

The Elephant Calf

Translated from the German by Gerhard Nellhaus

Edited by John Willett and Ralph Manheim

ARCADE PUBLISHING•NEW YORK

Copyright © 1927 by Arcadia Verlag, renewed 1968 by
Helene Brecht-Weigel
Translation copyright for the plays and texts by Brecht © 1979 by
Stefan S. Brecht
Introduction and editorial notes copyright © 1979 by Eyre Methuen Ltd.

All rights reserved. No part of this book may be reproduced in any form
or by any electronic or mechanical means, including information storage
and retrieval systems, without permission in writing from the publisher,
except by a reviewer who may quote brief passages in a review.

FIRST ARCADE PAPERBACK EDITION 2000

Man Equals Man and *The Elephant Calf,* originally published in German
under the titles *Mann ist Mann* and *Der Elefantenkalb* respectively,
were first published in this translation in 1979.

ISBN 1-55970-501-9
Library of Congress Catalog Card Number 99-59183
Library of Congress Cataloging-in-Publication information is available.

Published in the United States of America by Arcade Publishing, Inc.,
New York
Distributed by Time Warner Trade Publishing

10 9 8 7 6 5 4 3 2 1

CCP

PRINTED IN THE UNITED STATES OF AMERICA

CAUTION

These plays are fully protected by copyright. All inquiries concerning
the rights for professional or amateur stage production should be made
to Jerold L. Couture, Fitelson, Lasky, Aslan, and Couture, 551 Fifth
Avenue, New York, NY 10176. Inquiries concerning the rights for
professional stage production outside of the United States of America
should be directed to the International Copyright Bureau Ltd., 22a
Aubrey House, Maida Avenue, London W2 1TQ, England, and those
for amateur stage production to Samuel French Ltd., 2 Fitzroy Street,
London, W1P 6JR, England. Inquiries about use of any material other
than in performance should be directed to the publishers.

Contents

Introduction

This is the play of which Brecht said 'From what I learnt from the audiences that saw it, I rewrote *Man equals Man* ten times.' Nearly all Brecht's plays were copiously revised, while there are two or three great unfinished works which he tussled with for years, leaving a mountain of paper for his interpreters to sort out as best they can. But of the completed plays only *Galileo* and *The Good Person of Szechwan* preoccupied him to anything like the same extent as this quite early piece. He wrote it over a period during which he was evolving rapidly, as was the whole German theatre of the time and (for better or worse) the Weimar Republic under which that theatre so flourished. And so, for all its surface flippancies, it may well be of lasting importance for the understanding of Brecht and his age. It is at once a vital piece of theatre and something like an archaeological site.

He started planning it when he was still a twenty-year-old student oscillating between Augsburg and Munich around the time of the end of the First World War. Two years later his early diaries show that he was writing the odd scene, very much in the spirit of his Augsburg poems:

> Galgei was a solid citizen
> His head was rather thick.
> Some villains told him that he was
> The butter merchant Pick.

> They were such wicked people
> To play this dirty trick.
> Reluctantly he in the end
> Became the wicked Pick.

> How could he prove he wasn't?
> God left him high and dry.
> His catechism hadn't told
> Him he was named Galgei.

> The name might come in church lists
> Or on his tomb perhaps?
> The name Galgei however
> Could be some other chap's.
>
> Citizen Joseph Galgei
> Born April '83
> Devout and neat and honest
> As God likes men to be.

So his original concept of a worthy Augsburg citizen persuaded to lose his own identity in favour of that of a missing butter merchant had something of the quality of his one-act farces at that time: of *Lux in Tenebris* and the other Bavarian sketches which he is thought to have written under the impact of the great Munich clown Karl Valentin. But before he had got very far with it *Drums in the Night* took priority, followed by *In the Jungle of Cities* which he started in the autumn of 1921, around the time of his first long visit to Berlin.

The Augsburg *Galgei* play, then, went into cold storage throughout the period of his first Munich successes. This was a time during which the German Expressionist theatre was expiring, along with the Expressionist element in Brecht's own writing. When finally he moved to Berlin for good in the late summer of 1924 his work already had a much more urban, industrialised flavour to it – the transitional poem 'Of Poor BB' being crucial here – but *Galgei* was still high on the list of the tasks he had set himself. So too were a 'Mahagonny opera' and a vast plan for an urban trilogy of which *In the Jungle* would be the first section. The trilogy ran into difficulties, partly because the second play proved unexpectedly hard to write, but partly too, no doubt, because the production of *In the Jungle* with which the Deutsches Theater, Berlin, introduced its new dramaturg that October was not a success. At the same time his publisher was pressing him to complete his first book of poems, the *Devotions*, which he had promised them at least two years earlier, and to that end supplied him with an assistant called Elisabeth Hauptmann. It seems to have been her arrival, combined with the lack of any serious work to do at the Deutsches Theater, that decided the way in which he now set about *Galgei*, renaming it *Galy Gay oder Mann = Mann*.

In its second stage, then, *Man equals Man*, as we have called it, emerged not only as the first real product of Brecht's Berlin period but also as the first work of what became known as the 'Brecht collective' – that shifting group of friends and collaborators on whom he henceforward depended. As such it mirrored the artistic climate of the middle 1920s, with their attitude of 'Neue Sachlichkeit' (or New Matter-of-Factness), their stressing of the collectivity and downplaying of the individual, and their new cult of Anglo-Saxon imagery and sport. For along with Hauptmann now came a medical student from Munich, a protégé of Lion Feuchtwanger's called Emil Hesse Burri, who had acted as a second to the German middleweight champion Paul Samson-Körner, sparred with other leading boxers and himself wrote a play called *Tim O'Mara* (or *American Youth*). Brecht too became a friend of the champion and began ghosting his reminiscences for him under the title *The Human Fighting-Machine*, parts of which appeared in *Scherls Magazin* as did his boxing story 'Hook to the Chin'. Together the 'collective' would go to fights, not only absorbing their terminology and ethos (which permeates much of *Man equals Man*) but also drawing those conclusions for the theatre as a whole which Brecht set down in his theoretical essay 'Emphasis on Sport' and tried to realise by means of the harsh lighting, the boxing-ring stage and other anti-illusionistic devices that henceforward appeared in his own productions. Nothing could be less like the passionate, intensely egocentric gloom of so many Expressionist plays.

But there was another, perhaps even more important new element involved in Brecht's changed approach to the *Galgei* project. This lay most obviously in the shedding of the original Bavarian background and the shifting of the basic theme of human identity to a new setting in British India, something that German audiences even today must find utterly exotic. The precedent here was of course the Chicago background adopted for *In the Jungle*; and the inspiration quite clearly came from Kipling, who had already played a rather more marginal part in the mishmash of literary influences that went to make up the earlier play. Thus the three soldiers who transform Galy Gay into their fourth man recall the classic 'soldiers three'; the temple episode seems to echo the short story 'Krishna Mulvaney'; the song 'Johnny' is the old Boer War song 'Pack your kit and trek' which Kipling cites in 'Song of the Banjo'. And Brecht's own songs too – both the Man equals Man song of the early versions and the Widow Begbick song – are redolent of Kipling (as our translation tries to bring out). This affinity was already there before Brecht's move to Berlin, though at that point he had read Kipling only in German translation. But Hauptmann had studied English and acquired a real feeling for the language, and with her arrival the Kipling ties became more authentic. Nothing perhaps is more amazing to the English reader today than the quality of the soldiers' language. And it is instructive to see how it accords with the echoes from Hašek's novel, *The Good Soldier Schweik*, whose German translation had just appeared.

*   *   *

At the end of 1925 Brecht had the finished typescript bound up in red leather and gave it to 'Bess Hauptmann'. 'It was a troublesome play,' said his covering note,

> and even piecing together the manuscript from 20 lb of paper was heavy work; it took me 2 days, $\frac{1}{2}$ bottle of brandy, 4 bottles of soda water, 8–10 cigars and a lot of patience, and it was the only part I did on my own.

Up to that moment it seems that there had been no definite prospect of a production, and the result was an enormously unwieldy play, in which the whole of *The Elephant Calf*, virtually as we now have it, formed the penultimate scene. Then in the course of 1926 two provincial theatres decided to stage it, and in the spring Brecht and Hauptmann reworked it yet again ('for the seventh time, I think', said her diary for 30 April, 'and some scenes even more than that'). The result was the 1926 version which Ullstein, now Brecht's publisher, issued in book form the following year and which (being in the public domain) forms the basis of the English translation published by Grove Press in 1961 and subsequently adapted by Eric Bentley. It, as far as can be seen, is the text actually performed at the double première, which took place at Darmstadt and Düsseldorf on 25 September 1926. By then Brecht had been without regular employment for a year, while Hauptmann had gone on working for him for nothing after the previous publisher's commission had run out.

The Düsseldorf production fell flat, but Darmstadt (which is only some seventeen miles from Frankfurt) was another matter. Here the director of the former court theatre was Ernst Legal, a man who like his successor Carl Ebert was soon to move to a key position in Berlin; and he brought in two of Brecht's associates – the director Jacob Geis and the designer Caspar Neher – to take charge of the production, himself acting the part of Galy Gay. Visually it was most original: paper-thin, elegant, brilliantly lit with whites and khakis predominating; this was also the first time that Brecht's characteristic half-height curtain was used. Jazz music was played by Widow Begbick's three (subsequently eliminated) daughters. The Widow spoke her new Interlude speech with its key line 'Tonight you are going to see a man reassembled like a car.' And the critics came: not only Bernhard Diebold and Elisabeth Langgässer from Frankfurt, who were important enough, but also some of the influential men from Berlin, including Herbert Ihering and Alfred Kerr. Geis himself wrote in the Berlin theatre magazine *Die Szene* of his guiding aim

> to show the play's underlying sense by making the surface mean-ing as clear as possible. In other words, no implications, secrets, ambiguities, half-light; but facts, brilliant illumination, light into every corner, absence of feeling, no humour-with-a-catch-in-the-throat. The theatre considered as craft rather than art; avoidance of private affairs. These should make a secondary appearance, emerge as self-evident.

Though Geis advised them to get hold of this play the Berlin theatres were slow to take up the challenge. However, Alfred Braun's still quite new drama department at Radio Berlin was more enterprising, and in March 1927 it broadcast a radio adapta-tion specially made by Brecht. Introduced by a critical notice in *Der deutsche Rundfunk* (roughly equivalent to *The Listener*) which presented the play 'as the most powerful and original stage play of our time', this was linked by anonymous announcements which, again according to the same critic, were not merely

> a rehash of the stage directions in the book, but short sentences foretelling how the plot will develop, and reflecting something of the fairground barker's technique or the film titles of earlier times. Being written by a poet, these announcements give the whole evening a new form and one congenial to the radio medium.

The critic was Kurt Weill, whose first contact with Brecht and his work this seems to have been. The Galy Gay was again Legal, the Begbick Helen Weigel, taking her first step on the road that led to her Mother Courage some twenty years later. The music was by Edmund Meisel, Piscator's regular composer. The speech which

Brecht wrote to introduce the broadcast (see pp. 99–100) reappeared almost unchanged as his contribution to the first programme of Piscator's 1927–28 season, for which he was now acting as one of a 'collective' of dramaturgs. It shows him reconsidering the play in a new context of rapid technological advance, which seemed to demand just that malleability and relativity of human identity that its protagonist – for entirely different reasons – displays.

The published text of the play, which appeared the same year, reads like a shortened and somewhat subdued version of the 1924–25 script, with *The Elephant Calf* separated off as an appendix with the very Pirandellesque subtitle *or the Demonstrability of Any Conceivable Assertion*. The direction saying that this should be performed in the foyer only came later, nor does it ever seem to have been followed in Brecht's lifetime. This version also gives a melody and a piano accompaniment for the Man equals Man Song, (derived allegedly by Brecht and Hauptmann from *Madame Butterfly*), which subsequently disappeared from the play. Though it might have been expected that Piscator, who frequently complained about the dearth of plays for his new company, would give it its Berlin première, there is no sign that he even considered this; nor did he ever himself direct a Brecht work before 1945. On the contrary, it was Piscator's rivals and former employers at the Volksbünne who next staged it, in January 1928, using Neher once again as the designer, directed by another kindred spirit, Erich Engel. Heinrich George was the Galy Gay, with Weigel as a shingled, raucous-voiced Begbick in riding breeches and boots. It looks as though the text this time was severely shortened, cutting out scenes 5 and 7 and rolling 4, 6 and 8 together to make one long canteen scene; the play ended with scene 9. This, at least, is the case with the stage script which Arkadia, Ullstein's theatrical sudsidiary, subsequently put out.

The aim seems to have been to make this production more sharply anti-militarist, but it clearly did not satisfy Brecht. At the beginning of 1930, however, Leopold Jessner resigned as director of the Berlin Staatstheater – partly on account of the failure of a boxing play by Brecht's American friend Reyher, which Hauptmann had translated – and was succeeded by Legal, who must have had good memories of *Man equals Man* since he was quite willing to see it staged again. The surprising thing now was that in this time of economic cuts and incipient cultural conservatism he let it be directed by Brecht himself, whose long-standing ambition to

direct his own plays had generally been thwarted so far. The result
was that generally unpopular but highly original production of
February 1931 which was seen by the visiting Soviet playwright
Sergei Tretiakoff and 'produced a tremendous impression on
him', second only (he said) to that made by Meyerhold's 1922 production of *Le Cocu magnifique*.

> Giant soldiers armed to the teeth and wearing jackets caked
> with lime, blood and excrement stalk about the stage, holding
> on to wires to keep from falling off the stilts inside their trouser
> legs.

As indeed we see from the many surviving photographs, though
in fact only two of the three monsters were on stilts (the other
being grotesquely padded out) while the wires appear to be those
of the half-curtain in what was perhaps the lightest and subtlest of
all Caspar Neher's sets. Dwarfed by the soldiery, who already
seem a long way from Kipling, are the small figures of Weigel, as
a rather more mature and less masculine Begbick, and the round-
eyed Peter Lorre, the relatively obscure but greatly gifted young
actor who played Galy Gay.

So far as the text went two things distinguished Brecht's inter-
pretation at this time. First of all, he made Lorre deliver his
speeches in a broken, jerky manner, so as to emphasise the fact that
they were a stringing-together of contradictory passages, each
with its own specific attitude or 'gest'. (His answer to the critics
who took exception to this will be found on pp. 104–7.) Secondly
he yet again rewrote the play, this time with the advice of Dudow
and Bernhard Reich, basing himself on the Arkadia stage script
of 1930 and greatly reducing its more frivolous aspects. Thus
Begbick's daughters went out, as did the Man equals Man and
Drinking Truck songs with their Kipling echoes; Bloody Five too
became Germanised as the much less farcical-sounding Blutiger
Fünfer. For the production (though not for the version subsequently published) Begbick's Interlude speech was shifted to make
a prologue. Her 'Song of the Flow of Things' made its first appearance, closely recalling the 'Reader for Those Who Live in Cities'
poems which Brecht had written in 1926–27; so too did most of
the passages of spoken verse. This time Kurt Weill wrote the music,
which included a 'Nachtmusik' and a 'Schlacht-' (or Battle-)
'musik'. Unfortunately it disappeared after Hitler's advent to
power two years later, and has never since been found.

In 1938 the play was again published as part of the exiled Malik-Verlag's edition of Brecht's work, using a text evidently close to that of Brecht's production. It was never staged during the Nazi era, though there is an English version of scene 1 in Brecht's hand-writing dating from his years in California which suggests that he may have thought of doing something with it there; (this has been used, almost unamended. in our version since it sounds so like his authentic voice). Nor was it one of the plays which Brecht worked on with the Berliner Ensemble, so that it is difficult to tell how his final version might have turned out. What we now have in his German Collected Works (the basis for our edition) is the 1938 version as rather hurriedly amended when his German publishers began republishing the plays in the 1950s not long after his return to East Berlin. Here his account of his last amendments (as briefly resumed in the passage on p. 108) is not quite right. The two texts before him were those of the 1938 and 1926 editions, so what he did was to lop off the very end of scene 9 in the former, bring back scenes 10 and 11 (the train scene and the attack on the Tibetan fort) virtually as in the earlier version then round it off with Galy Gay's bloodthirsty verse speech much as before. He also once again appended *The Elephant Calf*, which had not been published at all in 1938. But none of this was tried out by him in the theatre, as he always wished before accepting a text as final.

*   *   *

To summarise this tangled story, so characteristic of Brecht's easily dissatisfied attitude to his own work, *Man equals Man* started out as a play about human malleability, lodged in the framework of an Augsburg farce. It was then bodily transported to Kipling's India, where it became more farcical still as well as a great deal more un-wieldy; touched with a Pirandello-like relativity and given some-thing of the tone of Hašek's *Schweik*. Brecht trimmed this version down in 1926, when it seemed closely in tune with the 'Neue Sachlichkeit' of the time: collectivist, unemotional, machine-con-scious, with elements of the music-hall and of circus clowning. Two years later, with the playwright becoming more socially aware, a serious purpose emerged: the farcical exotic soldiery proved to be licentious militarists set on their evil ends. Then came his alignment with the German Communist Party; but he was far too fond of this play to write it off as a youthful excess, and instead he brutalised the soldiers still further in order to make it primarily a statement against war and against colonial exploitation. For fifteen years after the publication of 1938 it slumbered, while Brecht lived through the most difficult period of his exile and wrote the big plays, from *Galileo* to *The Days of the Commune*: 'the dark times', as he termed them. At the end of it all, only three years or so before his death, he again tacked on the last two scenes of the 1926 version, with Bloody Five's self-castration and the Tibetan war, followed by the 1924–25 knockabout of the *Elephant Calf*. And so, to say the least, what we now have before us is an extremely inconsistent work.

All this is of course grist to the slow mills of what some term *Brechtforschung* and others, less flatteringly, 'the Brecht industry'; for students and scholars can spend happy hours trying to decide what Brecht really meant and at what point he meant it. The reader too can get considerable enjoyment from simply taking the end product as it comes, appendix and all; and if this is not enough there is some fairly amazing material in the notes (most of it not yet in the German editions). But for anybody wishing actually to perform the play the problem is not so easy. How are we to view anything so amorphous? Here the interpreters have differed widely, perhaps because so few have distinguished between the different layers making up the text as we now have it; thus it is not uncommon to find passages added in 1931 being taken virtually as the starting-point of the whole affair. Roughly speaking there seem to be three main approaches. One is to treat this play as the first true example of the 'epic theatre' advocated in Brecht's theoretical writings of the 1920s, and therefore as a significant piece of formal theatrical innovation. Another is to regard it as something of a confession: a denial of the importance of individual personality and specifically of Brecht's own, culminating in the episode where the sergeant castrates himself in a bloody parody of Lenz's *The Tutor*, an eighteenth-century play which Brecht was to adapt and stage much later. Finally there is the devoutly Marxist–Leninist view, according to which Galy Gay is a symbolic victim of capitalism, whom the British can turn into cannon-fodder because his job has infected him with petty-bourgeois values. He ends by being caught up in what Ernst Schumacher calls

> a piece of grisly colonial reality. The atrocities committed by colonial armies in Vietnam, Korea and other oppressed lands are still awaiting portrayal; or are they too great for any writer's imagination?

Far be it from us to tell potential directors which of the possible lines they should choose. For the play has not really got one; it is more a tangle of threads, each starting at a different point in the playwright's own evolution and each leading in a different direction. But there are certain things which should not be ignored. To start with, this is a play which is easily taken too solemnly (which is not the same thing as seriously), though the temptation is perhaps less in this country, where the irony and humour involved in Kipling's approach to British India are not always overlooked. Nor is there anything very new about its structure compared with the episodic form of Brecht's own earlier plays, or the use of acrobatic and music-hall methods by Eisenstein and others around 1922–23. The nature of its concern with 'personality' too can be misunderstood, for on the one hand the 1920s were a time of collective undertakings, even in the arts, where the ego had necessarily to make concessions, while on the other Brecht's specific *bête noire* – the notion of the *Charakterkopf* whose very features single him out as 'a personality' – probably goes back to some youthful irritation. Certainly it long antedated his first reading of Karl Marx, though the notion of the man who doesn't live but 'is lived' does indeed stem from his private, quasi-dialectical vision of the world as continually in flux. Why should identity itself not be part of that flux too?

The unreality of the colonial setting is self-evident: to Brecht Kilkoa, like the London of *The Threepenny Opera*, was simply a successful 'poetic conception', materialising out of his and Hauptmann's current reading rather than from the play's basic idea. Of course he then developed it and used it to launch his own attack on militarism and colonialism as the play proceeded, but this was something secondary, grafted-on, and to build it up into anything 'sharper' and more topical – with allusions to Rhodesia or whereever the next conflict may lie – risks making a monkey of the real anti-colonial cause. Certainly Brecht's own suggestion (p. 107) for making it more 'concretely' anti-Nazi would have been a disaster. For there is no getting over the underlying element of farce in this work. Right up to its final version much of it remains very funny, while the discarded material cited in our notes is often funnier still. Even if the director allows himself to treat this as the result of a philosophical concept of the Absurd rather than of Brecht's well-attested admiration for Karl Valentin and Chaplin, it is still difficult to damp it down. So the Berliner Ensemble, when they finally staged the play in a small-scale production by Uta Birnbaum, went a long way to do this aspect justice, turning the chassis of Begbick's truck into a trampoline with Ekkehard Schall as Bloody Five showing his great gifts as a solemn-faced clown.

The present edition is necessarily based on the 'final' text, though it is anybody's guess whether this is how Brecht would finally have left it if he could have staged it again after 1954. But it tries to give enough material – plans, jottings, explanatory notes and discarded passages or scenes – to let the reader follow the way in which Brecht pieced it together over the years. Even more than his other works, this play is a montage, the notion of montage indeed being its leit-motiv, determining not only its structure (particularly in the 'numbers' or 'turns' of scene 9) but also its treatment of the main character. We have also gone back to the earlier conception for the title, since *Man is Man* sounds somewhat German and *A Man's a Man*, though used on various occasions including our own parallel American edition, has a distracting echo of Robert Burns – who was not saying at all the same thing as Brecht. Instead we have taken the alternative title of the first Berlin version, which can also be found in Brecht's much later jottings, indicating that he retained some affection for it. For the play is a tale of equivalents. One man equals another: individuals can be swapped. One man equals no man: a man on his own is nothing, he needs to band together with others. Elephant equals elephant, never mind if it is a phoney. Blody Five equals Blody Five, till the squeak in his voice betrays the fact that he does not. And so on. Personality, in short, is less unique and important than we think. It can be manufactured or reassembled by society; it can be replaced. Now that the 'television personality' has come to seem as hollow a cliché as Brecht's Bavarian *Charakterkopf* this may again be a topical point.

THE EDITORS

Man equals Man

The transformation of the porter Galy Gay in the military cantonment of Kilkoa during the year nineteen hundred and twenty five

Collaborators: E. BURRI, S. DUDOW, E. HAUPTMANN, C. NEHER, B. REICH

Translators: GERHARD NELLHAUS and (for scene 1) BERTOLT BRECHT

Characters

URIAH SHELLEY
JESSE MAHONEY
POLLY BAKER
JERAIAH JIP
} *four privates in a machine-gun section of the British Army in India*

CHARLES FAIRCHILD, *known as Bloody Five, a Sergeant*
GALY GAY, *an Irish porter*
GALY GAY'S WIFE
MR WANG, *bonze of a Tibetan pagoda*
MAH SING, *his sacristan*
LEOKADIA BEGBICK, *canteen proprietress*
Soldiers

I

Kilkoa

Galy Gay and Galy Gay's wife

GALY GAY *sits one morning upon his chair and tells his wife*: Dear
wife, I have decided in accordance with our income to buy
a fish today. That would be within the means of a porter
who drinks not at all, smokes very little and has almost no
vices. Do you think I should buy a big fish or do you
require a small one?

WIFE: A small one.

GALY GAY: Of what kind should the fish be that you require?

WIFE: I would say a good flounder. But please look out for
the fishwives: they are lustful and always chasing men, and
you have a soft nature, Galy Gay.

GALY GAY: That is true but I hope they would not bother
with a penniless porter from the harbour.

WIFE: You are like an elephant which is the unwieldiest
beast in the animal kingdom, but he runs like a freight
train once he gets started. And then there are those soldiers
who are the worst people in the world and who are said to
be swarming at the station like bees. They are sure to be
hanging around in numbers at the market place and you
must be thankful if they don't break in and murder people.
What's more they are dangerous for a man on his own
because they always go around in fours.

GALY GAY: They would not want to harm a simple porter
from the harbour.

WIFE: One can never tell.

GALY GAY: Then put the water on for the fish, for I am
beginning to get an appetite and I guess I shall be back in
ten minutes.

2

Street outside the Pagoda of the Yellow God

Four soldiers stop outside the pagoda. Military marches are heard as troops move into the town.

JESSE: Party, halt! Kilkoa! This here is Her Majesty's town of Kilkoa where they are concentrating the army for a long-predicted war. Here we are, along with a hundred thousand other soldiers, all of us thirsting to restore order on the northern frontier.

JIP: That demands beer. *He collapses.*

POLLY: Just as the powerful tanks of our Queen must be filled with petrol if we are to see them rolling over the damned roads of this oversized Eldorado so can the soldier only function if he drinks beer.

JIP: How much beer have we left?

POLLY: There are four of us. We still have fifteen bottles. So we must get hold of another twenty-five bottles.

JESSE: That demands money.

URIAH: Some people object to soldiers, but just one pagoda like this contains more copper than a strong regiment needs to march from Calcutta to London.

POLLY: Our friend Uriah's suggestion with respect to a pagoda which, though rickety and covered with flyshit, may well be bursting with copper surely merits our sympathetic attention.

JIP: All I know, Polly, is I've got to have more to drink.

URIAH: Calm down, sweetheart. This Asia has a hole for us to crawl through.

JIP: Uriah, Uriah, my mother always used to say: Do what you like, my darlingest Jeraiah, but remember pitch always sticks. And this place stinks of pitch.

JESSE: The door isn't properly shut. Watch out, Uriah, you bet there's some devilry behind it.

URIAH: Nobody's going through this open door.

JESSE: Right, what are windows for?

URIAH: Take your belts and make a long line to fish for the collection boxes with. That's it.

They attack the windows. Uriah smashes one, looks inside and starts fishing.

POLLY: Catch anything?

URIAH: No, but my helmet's fallen in.

JESSE: Bloody hell, you can't go back to camp with no helmet.

URIAH: Oh boy, am I catching things! This is a shocking establishment. Just look. Snares. Mantraps.

JESSE: Let's pack it in. This isn't an ordinary temple, it's a trap.

URIAH: Temple equals temple. I've got to get my helmet out of there.

JESSE: Can you reach it?

URIAH: No.

JESSE: Perhaps I can get this latch to lift.

POLLY: Don't damage the temple, though.

JESSE: Ow! Ow! Ow!

URIAH: What's up now?

JESSE: Hand's got stuck.

POLLY: Let's call it off.

JESSE *indignantly*: Call it off? I need my hand back.

URIAH: My helmet's in there too.

POLLY: Then we'll have to go through the wall.

JESSE: Ow! Ow! Ow! *He pulls his hand out. It is covered with blood.* They'll have to pay for this hand. I'm not calling it off after that. Give us a ladder, come on!

URIAH: Wait! Hand over your paybooks first. A soldier's paybook must never be damaged. You can replace a man anytime, but a paybook is sacred if anything is.

They hand over their paybooks to him.

POLLY: Polly Baker.

JESSE: Jesse Mahoney.

JIP *crawling up*: Jeraiah Jip.

URIAH: Uriah Shelley. All from the Eighth Regiment. Stationed at Kankerdan, machine-gun section. Shooting will be avoided so that no visible damage is done to the temple. Forward!

Uriah, Jesse and Polly climb into the pagoda.

JIP *calls after them*: I'll mount guard. Then at least I won't have gone in. *The yellow face of Wang, the bonze, appears at a small window above.* How do you do? Are you the honourable owner? Delightful part of the world, this.

URIAH *within*: Hand me your knife, Jesse, so I can force these collection boxes open.

Wang smiles, and Jip smiles too.

JIP *to the bonze*: It is just awful, belonging to a troupe of hippopotamuses like that. *The face disappears.* Come on out. There's a man wandering around upstairs.

Electric bells are heard at intervals within.

URIAH: Watch where you step. What is it, Jip?

JIP: A man upstairs.

URIAH: A man? Everybody out! Hoy!

THE THREE *within, shouting and cursing*: Get your foot out of the way! – Let go! Now I can't move my foot. My boot's gone too – Don't weaken, Polly. Never! – It's my tunic now, Uriah! – What's a tunic? This temple must be wiped out. Now what? – Bloody hell, my trousers are stuck. That's what comes of being in a hurry. That idiot Jip.

JIP: Find anything? Whisky? Rum? Gin? Brandy? Ale?

JESSE: Uriah's ripped his trousers on a bamboo hook, and the boot on Polly's good foot is stuck in a mantrap.

POLLY: And Jesse's tangled up in electric wire.

JIP: That's just what I expected. Next time you go into a building why not use the front door?

Jip goes in through the door. The three climb out above, pale, bleeding and ragged.

POLLY: This calls for vengeance.

URIAH: This temple doesn't fight fair. Filthy, I call it.

POLLY: I want to see blood.

JIP *from within*: Hey!

POLLY *bloodthirstily advances on to the roof, but his boot gets stuck*: Now my other boot's gone.

URIAH: Now I shall shoot the place up.

The three climb down and aim their machine-gun at the pagoda.

POLLY: Fire!

They fire.

JIP *within*: Ow! What are you doing?

The three look up, horrified.

POLLY: Where are you?

JIP *within*: Here. You've gone and shot me through the finger.

JESSE: What the devil are you up to in that rat trap, you fool?

JIP *appearing in the doorway*: I wanted to get the money. Here it is.

URIAH *joyfully*: Trust the biggest rumpot of us all to get it first go off. *Aloud*: Come out of that door at once.

JIP *sticks his head out of the door*: Where did you say?

URIAH: Out of that door at once!

JIP: Oh, what's this?

POLLY: What's up with him?

JIP: Look!

URIAH: Now what?

JIP: My hair! Oh, my hair! I can't go forwards and I can't go back! Oh, my hair! It's stuck fast to something. Uriah, see what's sticking to my hair. Oh, Uriah, get me free! I'm hanging by the hair.

Polly tiptoes over to Jip and looks down at his hair.

POLLY: His hair is stuck to the door frame.

URIAH *shouts*: Your knife, Jesse, so as I can cut him free!

Uriah cuts him free, Jip lurches forward.

POLLY *amused*: And now he's got a bald patch.

They examine Jip's head.

JESSE: A bit of the skin came off too.

URIAH *looks at the two of them, then icily*: A bald patch will
give us away.

JESSE *with a venomous look*: A walking 'Wanted' notice!
Uriah, Jesse and Polly confer among themselves.

URIAH: We'll go back to camp and get a pair of scissors, then
come back this evening and crop all his hair off so the bald
patch can't be seen. *He gives back the paybooks.* Jesse Mahoney!

JESSE *taking his paybook*: Jesse Mahoney!

URIAH: Polly Baker!

POLLY *taking his paybook*: Polly Baker!

URIAH: Jeraiah Jip! *Jip tries to get up.* I'll hold on to yours.
He points to a palanquin in the courtyard. Sit in that leather box
and wait till dark.
*Jip crawls into the palanquin. The other three walk off dejectedly
shaking their heads. When they have left, Wang the bonze appears
in the doorway of the pagoda and takes some of the hair stuck to it
which he examines.*

3

Country Road between Kilkoa and the Camp

*Sergeant Fairchild appears from behind a shed and nails a poster to
it.*

FAIRCHILD: It is many moons since I, Bloody Five, known
also as Tiger of Kilkoa, the Human Typhoon, a sergeant
in the British Army, experienced anything as marvellous
as this. *Points at the poster.* Pagoda of the Yellow God broken
into. Roof of said Pagoda riddled with bullets. What have
we in the way of a clue? Four ounces of hair stuck to pitch.
If the roof is riddled with bullets then there must be a
machine-gun section involved; if there are four ounces of
hair at the scene of the crime then there must be a man who

is four ounces short. So if there is a machine-gun section containing a man with a bald patch then those are the offenders. It is all plain as a pikestaff. But who is this coming? *He steps behind the shed. The three approach and observe the poster with alarm. Then they go dejectedly on their way. But Fairchild appears from behind the shed and blows a police whistle. They stop.*

FAIRCHILD: Have none of you seen a man with a bald patch?

POLLY: No.

FAIRCHILD: Just look at you. Take your helmets off. Where is your fourth man?

URIAH: Why, Sergeant, he's relieving himself.

FAIRCHILD: Then we'll just wait for him and find out if he has seen a man with a bald patch. *They wait.* He seems to take a lot of relieving.

JESSE: Yes, sergeant.

They go on waiting.

POLLY: Perhaps he went a different way?

FAIRCHILD: It would be better for you, let me tell you, if you had summarily shot one another in your mothers' wombs than if you turn up at my roll call tonight without your fourth man. *Exit.*

POLLY: Let's hope that wasn't our new sergeant. If that rattle-snake is taking tonight's roll-call we might as well line up against the wall straight away.

URIAH: Before they sound the roll-call we'll have to have a fourth man.

POLLY: Here's a man coming now. Let's have a quiet look at him. *They hide behind the shed. Widow Begbick comes down the street. Galy Gay is following her, carrying her basket of cucumbers.*

BEGBICK: What are you moaning about? You're being paid by the hour, aren't you?

GALY GAY: That'll be three hours then.

BEGBICK: You'll get your money. This is a road that hardly anyone uses. A woman might have a hard time resisting a man that wished to embrace her.

GALY GAY: In your profession as a canteen owner always involved with soldiers, who are the worst people in the world, you must know certain holds.

BEGBICK: Ah, sir, you should never say such things to a woman. Certain words put women in a state when their blood gets aroused.

GALY GAY: I am only a simple porter from the harbour.

BEGBICK: It will be roll-call for the new lot in a few minutes. You can hear the drums already. At this hour there's not a soul on the road.

GALY GAY: If it's really as late as all that I'll have to turn around and hurry back to the town of Kilkoa, for I still have a fish to buy.

BEGBICK: Would you mind my asking you, Mr – I hope I've got the name correctly – Galy Gay, whether the profession of porter demands exceptional strength?

GALY GAY: I could never have imagined that unforeseen events would once again delay me for almost four hours from quickly buying fish and returning home, but I run like an express train once I get started.

BEGBICK: Yes, there is quite a difference between buying a fish to eat and helping a lady to carry her basket. But possibly the lady might be in a position to express her gratitude in a manner that would be more enjoyable than the eating of a fish.

GALY GAY: I must confess I would like to go and buy a fish.

BEGBICK: How can you be such a materialist?

GALY GAY: You know, I am a funny sort of person. Sometimes I know even before I get up: today I want a fish. Or I want a curry. When that happens the world can come to an end, but I just have to get a fish or a curry as the case may be.

BEGBICK: I understand, sir. But isn't it too late? The shops are closed and they are out of fish.

GALY GAY: You see, I am a man with great powers of imagination; I get fed up with a fish, for instance, even before I have set eyes on it. People set out to buy a fish, and first of all they buy that fish and secondly they carry that fish home, and thirdly they cook that fish till it is done, and fourthly they devour that fish, then at night after they have drawn a thick black line under their digestion they are still preoccupied with the same depressing fish, just because they are the sort who have no power of imagination.

BEGBICK: I see, you're only thinking of yourself all the time. *Pause.* Hm. If you are only thinking of yourself I suggest you take your fish money and buy this cucumber, which I will let you have as a favour. The cucumber is worth more, but you can keep the difference in return for carrying my basket.

GALY GAY: But I do not require a cucumber.

BEGBICK: I would never have expected you to humiliate me so.

GALY GAY: It is just that the water for the fish has already been put on.

BEGBICK: I see. Have it your own way. Have it your own way.

GALY GAY: No, no, believe me, I'd be only too glad to oblige you.

BEGBICK: Not another word, talking only makes it worse.

GALY GAY: Far be it from me to disappoint you. If you are still prepared to let me have the cucumber, here is the money.

URIAH *to Jesse and Polly*: That is a man who can't say no.

GALY GAY: Careful, there are soldiers about.

BEGBICK: God knows what they are doing around here at this hour. It is almost time for roll-call. Quick, hand me my basket, why should I go on wasting any more time standing here gossipping with you? But I would be happy to welcome you as a visitor to my beer waggon at the camp, for I am the widow Begbick, and my beer waggon is famous from Hyderabad to Rangoon. *She takes her packages and leaves.*

URIAH: That's our man.

JESSE: Someone who can't say no.

POLLY: And he even has red hair like old Jip.

The three set out.

JESSE: Nice evening tonight.

GALY GAY: Yes, sir.

JESSE: It's a funny thing, sir, but something tells me you come from Kilkoa.

GALY GAY: Kilkoa? Why, yes. That's where my cabin is, so to speak.

JESSE: I'm exceptionally glad to hear that, Mr . . .

GALY GAY: Galy Gay.

JESSE: You've got a cabin there, haven't you?

GALY GAY: Oh, have you met me already, as you know that? Or my wife perhaps?

JESSE: You're called, why yes, you're called . . . half a moment . . . Galy Gay.

GALY GAY: Perfectly true, that's my name.

JESSE: I knew it right away. You see, that's the way I am. For instance, I bet you're married. But why are we standing around like this, Mr Galy Gay? These are my friends Polly and Uriah. Won't you smoke a pipe with us in our canteen?

Pause. Galy Gay looks at them suspiciously.

GALY GAY: Many thanks. Unfortunately my wife is waiting for me in Kilkoa. Besides, I haven't personally got a pipe, absurd as that may seem to you.

JESSE: A cigar then. No, you can't refuse, it's such a nice evening.

GALY GAY: Well, in that case I can't say no.

POLLY: And you shall have your cigar.

Exeunt all four.

4

Canteen of the Widow Leokadja Begbick

Soldiers are singing 'The Song of Widow Begbick's Drinking Truck'.

SOLDIERS:

In Widow Begbick's drinking truck
You smokes and swigs and sleeps your time away.
You buys your beer and tries your luck
From Jubbulpore to Mandalay.
  From Halifax to Hindustan
  Horse, foot and guns, the service man
  Wants what the widow has to sell.
  It's toddy, gum and hi, hi, hi
  Bypassing heaven and skirting hell.
  Shut your big mouth, Tommy, keep your hair on, Tommy
  As you slide down Soda Mountain into Whisky Dell.

In Widow Begbick's drinking tank
You always gets the things that you likes best.
That's where the Indian Army drank
When you was drinking at Mummy's breast.
  From Halifax to Hindustan
  Horse, foot and guns, the service man
  Wants what the widow has to sell.
  It's toddy, gum and hi, hi, hi
  Bypassing heaven and skirting hell.
  Shut your big mouth, Tommy, keep your hair on, Tommy
  As you slide down Soda Mountain into Whisky Dell.

And when it's war in Cooch Behar
We'll stock ourselves with gum and smokes and beer

And climb on Begbick's drinking car
To show those wogs who's master here.
  From Halifax to Hindustan
  Horse, foot and guns, the service man
  Wants what the widow has to sell.
  It's toddy, gum and hi, hi, hi
  Bypassing heaven and skirting hell.
  Shut your big mouth, Tommy, keep your hair on,
    Tommy
  As you slide down Soda Mountain into Whisky Dell.

BEGBICK *entering*: Good evening, you military gentlemen. I
  am the Widow Begbick and this is my beer waggon which
  gets hooked on to the great troop trains and goes rolling
  over the entire Indian railway system; and because you
  can travel and drink beer and sleep in it at one and the same
  time it is called 'Widow Begbick's Beer Waggon' and everybody from Hyderabad to Rangoon knows that it has been
  a refuge to many an affronted soldier.
  *In the doorway stand the three soldiers with Galy Gay. They
  thrust him back.*
URIAH: Is this the Eighth Regiment canteen?
POLLY: Are we addressing the owner of the canteen, the
  world-famous Widow Begbick? We are the machine-gun
  section of the Eighth Regiment.
BEGBICK: Only three of you? Where is your fourth man?
  *They enter without answering, pick up two tables and carry them
  to the left where they build a kind of partition. The other soldiers
  look on in astonishment.*
JESSE: What kind of a man is the sergeant?
BEGBICK: Not nice.
POLLY: It is most disagreeable that the sergeant should not
  be nice.
BEGBICK: They call him Bloody Five, alias The Tiger of
  Kilkoa, the Human Typhoon. He has an unnatural sense
  of smell, he can smell criminal activity.

Jesse, Polly and Uriah look at one another.

URIAH: Indeed.

BEGBICK *to her guests*: This is the famous MG section which swung the battle of Hyderabad and is known as The Shower.

SOLDIERS: From now on they're part of our lot. Their crimes are said to follow them like shadows. *A soldier brings in a 'Wanted' notice which he nails up.* And right on their tail comes another of those signs.
The guests have stood up and slowly leave the canteen. Uriah whistles.

GALY GAY *entering*: I've been to this kind of establishment before. Printed menus. They have a whopping one at the Siam Hotel, gold on white. I bought one once. If you've got the right contacts you can get anything. One thing on it is Chicauqua sauce. And that's just a side dish. Chicauqua sauce!

JESSE *pushing Galy Gay towards the partition*: My dear sir, you are in a position to do three poor soldiers in distress a little service with no inconvenience to yourself.

POLLY: Our fourth man has been delayed taking leave of his wife, and if there are not four of us at roll-call we shall all be thrown into the black dungeons of Kilkoa.

URIAH: So it would help if you would put on one of our uniforms. You'd only need to be present when they number off the new arrivals and answer to his name. Just to keep the record straight.

JESSE: That's all.

POLLY: A cigar more or less that you might feel like smoking at our expense would not be worth mentioning.

GALY GAY: It is not that I am reluctant to oblige you, but unfortunately I have to hurry home. I have bought a cucumber for dinner and therefore cannot do exactly as I would like.

JESSE: Thank you. Frankly, it is what I expected of you. That's the point: you cannot do exactly as you would like.

You would like to go home, but you cannot. Thank you, sir, for justifying the confidence we placed in you the instant we set eyes on you. Your hand, sir.

He seizes Galy Gay's hand. Uriah motions him imperiously to go into the corner behind the tables. As soon as he is in the corner all three rush him and undress him except for his shirt.

URIAH: Permit us, for the said purpose, to clothe you in the noble garb of the glorious British Army. *He rings. Begbick appears.* Widow Begbick, can a man speak freely in these parts? We need a complete uniform. *Begbick produces a box and tosses it to Uriah. Uriah throws it to Polly.*

POLLY *to Galy Gay*: Here is the noble garb we purchased for you.

JESSE *showing him the trousers*: Put this garb on, brother Galy Gay.

POLLY *to Begbick*: It's because he lost his uniform.

The three of them dress Galy Gay.

BEGBICK: I see. He lost his uniform.

POLLY: Yes, a Chinese in the bath house managed to abstract our friend Jip's service dress.

BEGBICK: I see: in the bath house?

JESSE: As a matter of fact, Widow Begbick, we're having a bit of a lark.

BEGBICK: I see: a lark?

POLLY: Isn't that right, my dear sir? Isn't it all a bit of a lark?

GALY GAY: Yes, it's a sort of a bit of a – cigar. *He laughs.* *The three laugh too.*

BEGBICK: How helpless a weak woman is against four such strong men. Let no one ever say the Widow Begbick hindered a man from changing his trousers.

She goes to the rear and writes on a slate: 1 pair of trousers, 1 tunic, 1 pair of puttees etc.

GALY GAY: What's all this about?

JESSE: It's all about nothing, really.

GALY GAY: Won't it be dangerous if it gets found out?

POLLY: Not in the least. And in your case, once equals never.

GALY GAY: True enough. Once equals never. Or so they say.

BEGBICK: That uniform will be five shillings an hour.

POLLY: Sheer bloody extortion, three's the limit.

JESSE *at the window*: Rain clouds are coming up fast. If it rains now the palanquin will get wet, and if the palanquin gets wet they'll take it into the pagoda, and if they take it into the pagoda Jip will be discovered, and if Jip is discovered we're sunk.

GALY GAY: Too small. I'll never get into it.

POLLY: You see, he can't get into it.

GALY GAY: And the boots pinch horribly.

POLLY: Everything's too small. Unusable! Two bob.

URIAH: Shut up, Polly. Four bob because everything's too small and particularly because the boots pinch so. Don't they?

GALY GAY: To the highest degree. They pinch quite particularly.

URIAH: The gentleman isn't such a crybaby as you, you see, Polly.

BEGBICK *comes up to Uriah, leads him to the rear and points at the 'Wanted' sign*: This poster has been up all round the camp for the last hour, stating that a military crime has been perpetrated in this town. The guilty parties have not yet been identified. And if the uniform costs no more than five shillings it's because I'm not having the whole company dragged into this crime.

POLLY: Four shillings is a lot of money.

URIAH *coming forward*: Be quiet, Polly. Ten bob.

BEGBICK: Anything that might besmirch the company's honour can generally be cleaned up in Widow Begbick's Drinking Car.

JESSE: By the way, Widow Begbick, do you think it'll rain?

BEGBICK: To answer that one I'd have to take a look at the sergeant, Bloody Five. It's well known throughout the army that when it rains he gets into the most appalling states of sensuality and is outwardly and inwardly transformed.

JESSE: You see, this lark of ours absolutely depends on its not raining.

BEGBICK: Not a bit of it. Once it starts raining Bloody Five, from being the most dangerous man in the British Army, becomes harmless as a kitten. As soon as he gets one of his fits of sensuality he is blind to everything going on around him.

A SOLDIER *calls into the room*: All out for roll call; it's that pagoda business, there's supposed to be a man missing. So they're calling the roll and checking paybooks.

URIAH: His paybook!

GALY GAY *kneels down and wraps up his old clothes*: I take good care of my things, you see.

URIAH *to Galy Gay*: Here's your paybook. All you have to do is to call out our comrade's name, very clearly and as loud as possible. Nothing to it.

POLLY: And our lost comrade's name is Jeraiah Jip. Jeraiah Jip!

GALY GAY: Jeraiah Jip!

URIAH *to Galy Gay as they walk off*: It's a pleasure to meet well-bred persons who know how to conduct themselves in any situation.

GALY GAY *stops just inside the door*: And what is in it for me?

URIAH: A bottle of beer. Come on.

GALY GAY: Gentlemen, my profession of porter obliges me to look after my own interests in any situation. I was thinking of two boxes of cigars and four or five bottles of beer.

JESSE: But we need you for that roll call.

GALY GAY: Exactly.

POLLY: All right. Two boxes of cigars and three or four bottles of beer.

GALY GAY: Three boxes and five bottles.

JESSE: I don't get it. You just said two boxes.

GALY GAY: If you're going to take that line it will be five boxes and eight bottles.

A bugle call.

URIAH: Time we were out of here.

JESSE: Right. It's a deal if you come along with us straight away.

GALY GAY: Right.

URIAH: And what is your name?

GALY GAY: Jip! Jeraiah Jip!

JESSE: So long as it doesn't rain.

POLLY *comes back; to Begbick*: Widow Begbick, we understand the sergeant becomes very sensual when it rains. And now it's going to rain. See to it that he's blind to whatever goes on around him for the next few hours, or else we risk getting found out. *Exit.*

BEGBICK *looking after them*: That man's not called Jip, I happen to know. That's a porter called Galy Gay from Kilkoa, and at this very instant a man who is by no means a soldier is forming up under the eyes of Bloody Five. *She takes a mirror and goes to the rear.* I'll stand here where Bloody Five is sure to see me, and lure him in.

Second bugle call. Enter Fairchild. Begbick looks at him seductively in the mirror and sits down in a chair.

FAIRCHILD: Don't cast such devouring glances at me, you white-washed Babylon. Things are bad enough already. Three days ago I took to my bunk and began washing in cold water. On Thursday my unbridled sensuality forced me to proclaim a state of siege against myself. It is a particularly disagreeable situation for me since only today I sniffed out a crime virtually without precedent in military history.

BEGBICK:

Follow, o Bloody Five, thine own great nature
Unobserved! For who will learn it?
And in the pit of my arm, in my hair
Learn who thou art. And in the crook of my knee forget

Thy fortuitous name.
Pathetic discipline! Poverty-stricken Order!
Therefore, Bloody Five, I entreat thee come
To me in this night of tepid rainfall
Exactly as thou fearest to: as man
A contradiction. As must-but-don't-want-to.
Come now as man. Just as nature made thee
With no tin hat. Confused and savage and tied up in thyself
And defenceless victim of thy instincts
And helpless slave of thine own strength.
Come, then, as man.

FAIRCHILD: Never. The collapse of Mankind started when the first of these Zulus left a button undone. The Infantry Training Manual is a book chock-a-block with weaknesses, but it is the one thing a man can fall back on, because it stiffens the backbone and takes over responsibility towards God. Verily a hole should be dug in the ground and dynamite put in it so as to blow up the entire planet; then they might just begin to realise one means business. It's all plain as a pikestaff. But will you, Bloody Five, be able to last out this rainy night without the widow's flesh?

BEGBICK: So when you come to me tonight I want you to wear a black suit and have a bowler hat on your head.

A VOICE OF COMMAND: Machine-gunners fall in for roll call!

FAIRCHILD: Now I must sit by this door post so as to keep an eye on this scum they're counting. *Sits down.*

VOICES OF THREE SOLDIERS *outside*: Polly Baker. – Uriah Shelley. – Jesse Mahoney.

FAIRCHILD: Ha, and now there will be a slight pause.

GALY GAY'S VOICE *outside*: Jeraiah Jip!

BEGBICK: Correct.

FAIRCHILD: They're up to something again. Insubordination without. Insubordination within. *He stands up and starts to leave.*

BEGBICK *calls after him*: But let me inform you, Sergeant, that before the black rains of Nepal have fallen for three nights you will take a more lenient view of human failings, for you are perhaps the most sex-ridden individual under the sun. You will hobnob with insubordination, and the desecrators of the temple will gaze deep into your eyes, for your own crimes will be as numberless as the sands of the sea.

FAIRCHILD: Ho, we'd take action in that case, my dear, believe me, we'd take action in exemplary fashion against that insubordinate little Bloody Five. The whole thing's plain as a pikestaff. *Exit.*

FAIRCHILD'S VOICE *outside*: Eight men up to the navel in hot sand for non-regulation haircuts!

Enter Uriah, Jesse and Polly with Galy Gay. Galy Gay steps forward.

URIAH: Scissors, please, Widow Begbick.

GALY GAY *to the audience*: This sort of little favour, man to man, can't do any harm. You scratch my back and I'll scratch yours, that's the idea. Now I'll drink a glass of beer as if it were water and tell myself: you've done these gentlemen a good turn. And all that counts in this world is to take a chance now and then and say 'Jeraiah Jip' the way another man would say 'Good evening', and be the way people want you to be, because it's so easy.

Begbick brings a pair of scissors.

URIAH: Time we looked for Jip.

JESSE: That's a nasty storm blowing up.

The three turn to Galy Gay.

URIAH: I am afraid we're in a great hurry, sir.

JESSE: We've still got to crop a gentleman's hair, you see.

They turn to the door. Galy Gay runs after them.

GALY GAY: Couldn't I help you with that too?

URIAH: No, we have no further need of you, sir. *To Begbick*: Five boxes of cheap cigars and eight bottles of brown ale for this man. *On the way out*: There are some people who will keep sticking their noses into everything. Give them a finger and they'll have your whole hand.

The three hurry out.

GALY GAY:

Now I could go away, but
Should a man go away when he is sent away?
Perhaps once he has gone
He may be needed again? And can a man go away
When he is needed. Unless it has to be
A man should not go away.

Galy Gay goes to the rear and sits down in a chair by the door. Begbick takes beer bottles and cigar boxes and places them in a circle on the ground in front of Galy Gay.

BEGBICK: Haven't we met somewhere? *Galy Gay shakes his head.* Aren't you the man who carried my basket of cucumbers for me? *Galy Gay shakes his head.* Isn't your name Galy Gay?

GALY GAY: No.

Exit Begbick shaking her head. It grows dark. Galy Gay falls asleep on his chair. Rain falls. Begbick is heard singing to soft music.

BEGBICK:

Often as you may see the river sluggishly flowing
Each time the water is different.
What's gone can't go past again. Not one drop
Ever flows back to its starting point.

5
Interior of the Pagoda of the Yellow God

Wang the bonze and his sacristan

SACRISTAN: It is raining.

WANG: Bring in our leather palanquin out of the rain. *The sacristan goes out.* Now the last of our takings have been stolen. And now the rain is coming in on my head through those bullet holes. *The sacristan drags in the palanquin. Groans from within.* What's that? *He looks inside.* I knew it must be a white man as soon as I saw what a disgusting state the palanquin was in. Oh, he's wearing a uniform. And he's got a bald spot, this thief. They've simply cut his hair off. What shall we do with him? Since he is a soldier he must be without brains. A soldier of his Queen, coated with sicked-up drinks, more helpless than an infant hen, too drunk to recognise his own mother. We can hand him to the police. What's the good of that? Once the money has gone what's the good of justice? And all he can do is grunt. *Furiously*: Heave him out, you cheese-hole, and stuff him in the prayer-box, but make sure his head is on top. Our best answer is to make a god of him. *The sacristan puts Jip into the prayer box.* Get me some paper. We must hang out paper flags at once. We must immediately paint posters for all we are worth. No false economies: I want it to be a big operation, with posters that can't be overlooked. What's the good of a god that doesn't get talked about? *A knock at the door.* Who is calling on me at this hour?

POLLY: Three soldiers.

WANG: Those will be his comrades. *He admits the three.*

POLLY: We are looking for a gentleman, or more specifically a soldier, who is sleeping in a leather box that once stood outside this rich and distinguished temple.

WANG: May his awakening be a pleasant one.

POLLY: That box however has disappeared.

WANG: I understand your impatience, which originates in uncertainty; for I too am looking for some men, about three all told, specifically soldiers, and I cannot find them.

URIAH: That will be extremely difficult. I'd say you might as well give up. But we thought you might know something about that leather box.

WANG: Unhappily not. The unpleasant fact is that all you honourable soldiers wear the same clothes.

JESSE: That is not unpleasant. Inside the said leather box just now is sitting a man who is very ill.

POLLY: Having moreover lost a certain amount of hair through his illness he is in urgent need of help.

URIAH: Might you have seen such a man?

WANG: Unhappily not. I did however find hair such as you mention. But a sergeant in your army took it away with him. He wished to give it back to the honourable soldier.

Jip groans inside the prayer box.

POLLY: What is that, sir?

WANG: That is my cow who is slumbering.

URIAH: Your cow does not seem to slumber very well.

POLLY: This is the palanquin we stuffed Jip into. Permit us to inspect it.

WANG: It will be best if I tell you the whole truth. It is not the same palanquin.

POLLY: It's as full of sick as a slop pail on the third day of Christmas. Jesse, it's obvious Jip was here.

WANG: He couldn't have been in that, now, could he? Nobody would get into such a filthy palanquin.

Jip groans loudly.

URIAH: We've got to have our fourth man. Even if it means murdering our own grandmother.

WANG: I fear the man you are looking for is not here. But to make it clear to you that the man who in your opinion is here but of whose presence I have no knowledge is not your man, allow me to explain the entire situation by means of a drawing. Permit your unworthy servant to delineate four criminals by means of chalk. *He draws on the door of the prayer box.*

One of them has a face, so you can see who he is, but three of them have no faces. You cannot recognise them. Now the man with the face has got no money, so he is not a thief. Those with the money however have got no faces, so you cannot know them. Unless they are together, that is. But once they are together the three faceless ones will grow faces, and other people's money will be found on them. You will never make me believe that a man who might be here is your man.

The three threaten him with their weapons, but at a sign from Wang the sacristan appears with Chinese worshippers.

JESSE: We shall not disturb your night's rest any longer, sir. Besides, your tea doesn't agree with us. Your drawing, to be sure, is very clever. Come along.

WANG: It grieves me to see you depart.

URIAH: Do you really believe that when our comrade wakes up, no matter where, wild horses will prevent him from coming back to us?

WANG: Wild horses possibly not, but a small portion of domestic horse, who knows?

URIAH: Once he's shaken the beer out of his head he'll be back. *The three leave amid deep bows.*

JIP *inside the prayer box*: Hey!

Wang draws the attention of the worshippers to his god.

6

The Canteen

Late at night. Galy Gay is sitting in his chair, still asleep. The three soldiers appear in the window.

POLLY: He's still sitting there. Like an Irish mammoth, isn't the?
URIAH: Perhaps he didn't want to leave on account of the rain.
JESSE: Who can say? Anyhow we're going to need him again now.
POLLY: Don't you think that Jip will be back?
JESSE: Uriah, I know that Jip will not be back.
POLLY: We can hardly tell this porter the same old tale again.
JESSE: What do you think, Uriah?
URIAH: I think I'll have a kip.
POLLY: But suppose this porter now gets up and walks out of that door our heads will be hanging by a mere thread.
JESSE: Definitely. But I'm turning in now too. You can't expect too much of a fellow.
POLLY: Perhaps it's best if we all have a kip. It's too depressing and it's really all the fault of the rain.
Exeunt the three.

7

Interior of the Pagoda of the Yellow God

Towards morning. Large posters on all sides. The sound of an old gramophone and of a drum. Religious ceremonies of some importance appear to be going on in the background.

WANG *approaches the prayer box; to the sacristan*: Roll those camel-dung balls quicker, you trash! *Close to the prayer box*: Is the honourable soldier still asleep?

JIP *inside*: Shall we be de-training soon, Jesse? This truck is shaking so dreadfully, and it's as cramped as a water closet.

WANG: Honourable soldier, you must not imagine that you are in a railway truck. If anything is shaking it is the beer in your honourable head.

JIP *inside*: Nonsense. Who's that singing in the gramophone? Can't it stop?

WANG: Come on out, honourable soldier, eat a piece of meat from a cow.

JIP *inside*: Is it all right for me to have a piece of meat, Polly? *He pounds on the sides of the prayer box.*

WANG *running to the rear*: Quiet, you wretches! The god you can hear knocking on the walls of the holy prayer box is asking for five taels. Grace is being shown unto you. Take a collection, Mah Sing.

JIP *inside*: Uriah, Uriah, where am I?

WANG: Knock a little more, honourable soldier, on the other wall, honourable general, with both your feet, emphatically.

JIP *inside*: Hey, what is this? Where am I? Where are you? Uriah, Jesse, Polly!

WANG: Your grovelling servant is desirous of knowing what food and strong drinks the honourable soldier wishes to call for.

JIP *inside*: Hey, who's that? What is that voice that sounds like a fat rat talking?

WANG: That moderately fat rat, colonel, is your friend Wang from Tientsin.

JIP *inside*: What town am I in now?

WANG: A wretched town, exalted patron, a hole known as Kilkoa.

JIP *inside*: Let me out!

WANG *to the rear*: When you have finished rolling the camel dung into balls, lay them out on a dish, beat the drum and light them. *To Jip*: At once, honourable soldier, if only you promise not to run away.

JIP *inside*: Open up, you voice of a muskrat, open up, do you hear!

WANG: Wait, wait, ye faithful! Stay where you are for just one instant. The god will speak to you in three thunderclaps. Count them carefully. Four, no, five. Too bad: he only wishes you to sacrifice five taels. *Taps on the prayerbox; in a friendly tone*: Honourable soldier, here is a beefsteak for your mouth.

JIP *inside*: Oh, now I feel it, my insides are utterly corroded. I must have rinsed them in pure alcohol. Oh, it may be that I have had too much to drink and now I am having to eat the same amount.

WANG: You may eat a whole cow, honourable soldier, and a beefsteak already awaits you. But I fear you will run away, honourable soldier. Do you promise me that you will not run away?

JIP *inside*: Let's have a look at it first. *Wang lets him out.* How did I get here?

WANG: Through the air, honourable general. You came through the air.

JIP: Where was I when you found me?

WANG: Deigning to rest in an old palanquin, Exalted One.

JIP: And where are my comrades? Where is the Eighth Regiment? Where is our machine-gun section? Where are those twelve troop trains and four elephant parks? Where is the whole British Army? Where have they all gone, you grinning yellow spittoon?

WANG: Somewhere beyond the Punjab Mountains a month ago. But here is a beefsteak.

JIP: What? And me? Where was I? What was I doing when they were moving off?

WANG: Beer, much beer, one thousand bottles, and making money too.

JIP: Didn't people come asking for me?

WANG: Unfortunately not.

JIP: That is disagreeable.

WANG: But if they should come now, looking for a man in the uniform of a white soldier, should I bring them to you, honourable Minister of War?

JIP: That is not necessary.

WANG: If you don't want to be disturbed, Johnny, just step into this box, Johnny, in case anyone comes who offends your eye.

JIP: Where's that beefsteak? *Sits down and eats.* It's far too small. What is that ghastly noise?
To the sound of drumming the smoke from the camel-dung balls rises to the ceiling.

WANG: That is the prayers of the faithful who are down on their knees back there.

JIP: It's from a tough part of the cow. Who are they praying to?

WANG: That is their secret.

JIP *eating more quickly*: This is a good beefsteak, but it is wrong that I should be sitting here. Polly and Jesse are sure to have waited for me. They may still be waiting. It's as soft as butter. It is bad of me to be eating. I can hear Polly telling Jesse: Jip will definitely be back. As soon as he's sobered up, Jip will be back. Uriah may not exactly burst himself waiting, because Uriah is a bad man, but Jesse and Polly will say: Jip will be back. No question but this is an appropriate meal for me after all that liquor. If only Jesse didn't have such blind faith in his old friend Jip; but as it is he's saying: Jip won't let us down, and of course that's hard for me to bear. It's all wrong that I should be sitting here, but this is good meat.

8

The Canteen

Early morning. Galy Gay is still asleep in his chair. The three are eating breakfast.

POLLY: Jip will be back.

JESSE: Jip won't let us down.

POLLY: As soon as he's sobered up, Jip will be back.

URIAH: You never can tell. Anyway we won't let this porter out of our hands so long as Jip is still out on the tiles.

JESSE: He never left.

POLLY: He must be frozen stiff. He spent the whole night on that wooden chair.

URIAH: But we had a good night's sleep and are in fine shape again.

POLLY: And Jip will be back. That much is clear to my sound, well-rested military mind. As soon as Jip wakes up he'll want his beer, and then Jip will be back.

Enter Wang. He goes to the bar and rings. Enter Widow Begbick.

BEGBICK: I'm not serving native undesirables, nor yellow ones neither.

WANG: For a white man: ten bottles of good light beer.

BEGBICK: For a white man ten bottles of light beer. *She gives him the ten bottles.*

WANG: Yes, for a white man. *Exit Wang, bowing to all. Jesse, Polly and Uriah exchange looks.*

URIAH: Jip won't be back now. We must take some beer on board. Widow Begbick, in future you will keep twenty beers and ten whiskies permanently at action stations. *Begbick pours beer and goes out. The three drink and observe the sleeping Galy Gay.*

POLLY: But how do we manage it, Uriah? All we have is Jip's paybook.

URIAH: That's enough. That'll give us a new Jip. People are taken much too seriously. One equals no one. Anything less than two hundred at a time is not worth mentioning. Of course anybody can be of a different opinion. An opinion is of no consequence whatever. Any level-headed man can level-headedly adopt two or three different opinions.

JESSE: They can stuff their 'personalities'.

POLLY: But what's he going to say if we turn him into Private Jeraiah Jip?

URIAH: His kind change of their own accord, you know. Throw him into a pond, and two days later he'll have webs growing between his fingers. That's because he's got nothing to lose.

JESSE: Never mind what he says, we've got to have a fourth man. Wake him up.

POLLY *wakes Galy Gay*: Dear sir, what a piece of luck that you didn't leave. Circumstances have arisen which prevented our friend Jeraiah Jip from reporting here on time.

URIAH: Are you of Irish extraction?

GALY GAY: I think so.

URIAH: That is a help. I trust you are not over forty, Mr Galy Gay?

GALY GAY: I am not as old as that.

URIAH: Brilliant. Have you by any chance got flat feet?

GALY GAY: Somewhat.

URIAH: That settles it. Your fortune is made. For the time being you can remain here.

GALY GAY: Unhappily my wife is expecting me in connection with a fish.

POLLY: We understand your hesitations: they are honourable and worthy of an Irishman. But we like your appearance.

JESSE: And what's more, it fits the bill. There may perhaps be an opening for you to become a soldier.
Galy Gay is silent.

URIAH: The soldier's life is extremely pleasant. Every week they give us a handful of money and all we have to do in return is to foot it round India gazing at these highways and pagodas. Kindly take a look at the comfortable leather sleeping bags that are issued to a soldier free of charge. Cast your eye on this rifle bearing the trademark of the firm of Everett and Co. Mostly we amuse ourselves fishing, with tackle bought for us by Mum, as we laughingly call the army, while a number of military bands take it in turn to provide music. For the remainder of the day you smoke in your bungalow or idly observe the golden palaces of one of those Rajahs, whom you may also shoot if you feel so inclined. The ladies expect a great deal from us soldiers, but never money, and that, you must admit, is yet another attraction. *Galy Gay is silent.*

POLLY: The soldier's life in wartime is particularly pleasant. Only in battle does a man attain his full stature. Do you realise that you are living in momentous times? Before each infantry attack the soldier is given a large glass of spirits free of charge, after which his courage is boundless, positively boundless.

GALY GAY: I realise that the soldier's life is a pleasant one.

URIAH: Definitely. So this means you can keep your military uniform with its pretty brass buttons and have a right to be called Mr at any moment: Mr Jip.

GALY GAY: You cannot wish to cause unhappiness to a poor porter.

JESSE: Why not?

URIAH: You mean you want to leave?

GALY GAY: Yes, I am leaving now.

JESSE: Polly, go and get his clothes.

POLLY *with the clothes*: What's the reason for your not wanting to be Jip, then?
Fairchild appears at the window.

GALY GAY: The fact that I am Galy Gay. *He goes to the door. The three look at one another.*

URIAH: Just wait a minute longer.

POLLY: Have you ever heard the saying: More haste, less speed?

URIAH: You are up against the sort of men who don't like accepting free gifts from strangers.

JESSE: Whatever your name is, you should get something for having been so obliging.

URIAH: It all boils down – all right, keep your hand on the doorknob – to a bit of business.

Galy Gay stops short.

JESSE: This bit of business is as good as anything Kilkoa has to offer, aren't I right, Polly? You know, if we could manage to get our hands on that . . .

URIAH: It is our duty to offer you a chance to get in on this stupendous bit of business.

GALY GAY: Business? Did I hear you say business?

URIAH: Possibly. But you've no time for that, have you?

GALY GAY: There's having time and having time.

POLLY: Oh, you'd have time all right. If you knew what this bit of business was you'd have time all right. After all, Lord Kitchener had time to conquer Egypt.

GALY GAY: I should think so. You mean it's a big bit of business?

POLLY: For the Maharajah of Peshawar it might be. But it might not be all that big perhaps for a big man like you.

GALY GAY: What would I have to contribute in this bit of business?

JESSE: Nothing.

POLLY: At the most you might have to sacrifice your moustache, which could possibly provoke undesirable notoriety.

GALY GAY: I see. *He takes his things and starts for the door.*

POLLY: What an utter elephant!

GALY GAY: Elephant? Elephants are a goldmine of course. If you've got an elephant you'll never end up in the workhouse. *Excitedly takes a chair and sits down in the centre of the group.*

URIAH: Elephant? You bet we've got an elephant.

GALY GAY: Would your elephant be such as to be instantly available?

POLLY: An elephant! That's something he seems extremely keen on.

GALY GAY: So you have an elephant available?

POLLY: Who ever heard of a bit of business involving an unavailable elephant?

GALY GAY: Well, in that case, Mr Polly, I too would be glad to get my cut of this.

URIAH *hesitantly*: The only trouble is the Devil of Kilkoa.

GALY GAY: The devil of Kilkoa, what's that?

POLLY: Speak quieter. You're speaking the name of the Human Typhoon, Bloody Five, our sergeant.

GALY GAY: What does he do to get such names?

POLLY: Oh, nothing. Occasionally when a man gives the wrong name at roll call he bundles him up in six feet of canvas and dumps him in among the elephants.

GALY GAY: So you need a man with a head on his shoulders.

URIAH: You have that head, Mr Galy Gay.

POLLY: A head like that has something in it.

GALY GAY: Nothing to speak of. But I do know a riddle that might be of interest to educated persons like yourselves.

JESSE: You are in fact surrounded by expert riddle-guessers.

GALY GAY: It goes like this: what's white, is a mammal, and can see as well behind as in front?

JESSE: That's a hard one.

GALY GAY: You'll never guess this riddle. I couldn't guess it myself. A mammal. White. Sees as well behind as in front. A blind white horse.

URIAH: It's a prodigious riddle.

POLLY: And you just keep all that in your head?

GALY GAY: As a rule, because I'm no good at writing. But I fancy I'm the right man for any bit of business.

The three go to the bar. Galy Gay takes a box of his cigars and hands it round.

URIAH: Matches!

GALY GAY *while lighting their cigars*: Gentlemen, permit me to prove to you that you have selected no bad associate for your bit of business. Do you happen to have some heavy objects handy?

JESSE *points to some weights and clubs lying along the wall by the door*: There you are.

GALY GAY *taking the heaviest weight and lifting it*: I'm a member of the Kilkoa Wrestling Club, you see.

URIAH *handing him a bottle of beer*: Anyone can tell that from the way you behave.

GALY GAY *drinking*: Yes, we wrestlers have our own way of behaving. There are certain rules. For instance, when a wrestler comes into a room full of people, he hoists his shoulders on entering, raises his arms to shoulder height, then lets them dangle and saunters into the room. *He drinks.* Join up with me and you can rob a bank.

FAIRCHILD *enters*: There's a woman out here who is looking for an individual called Galy Gray.

GALY GAY: Galy Gay! Galy Gay's the name of the individual she's looking for.

Fairchild looks at him for a moment, then fetches Mrs Galy Gay.

GALY GAY *to the three*: Don't worry, she's a gentle soul, being as how she's from a province where nearly everyone is friendly. You can rely on me. Galy Gay has tasted blood.

FAIRCHILD: Come in, Mrs Gray. There's a man here who knows your husband. *He comes back with Galy Gay's wife.*

MRS GALY GAY: Excuse a humble woman, gentlemen, and pardon the way I am dressed, I was in such a hurry. Ah, there you are, Galy Gay. But are you really you in that army uniform?

GALY GAY: No.

MRS GALY GAY: I can't make you out. How do you come to be in uniform? It doesn't suit you a bit, ask anybody. You're a strange man, Galy Gay.

URIAH: She isn't right in the head.

MRS GALY GAY: It's not easy being married to someone who cannot say no.

GALY GAY: I wonder who she's talking to.

URIAH: Sounds like insults to me.

FAIRCHILD: In my opinion Mrs Gray is extremely lucid in the head. Please go on talking, Mrs Gray. Your voice is more grateful to my ears than a coloratura soprano.

MRS GALY GAY: I don't know what you're up to this time with your big ideas, but you'll come to no good end. Come along now. Why don't you say something? Have you got a sore throat?

GALY GAY: I do believe you are addressing all that to me. You've mistaken me for someone else, let me tell you, and what you're saying about him is stupid and tactless.

MRS GALY GAY: What's that? Mistaken you? Have you been drinking? He can't stand drink, you see.

GALY GAY: I'm no more your Galy Gay than I'm the Army Commander.

MRS GALY GAY: I put the water on around this time yesterday, but you never brought the fish.

GALY GAY: What's this about a fish? You are talking as if you had lost your wits, and in front of all these gentlemen too!

FAIRCHILD: This is a most remarkable case. It conjures up such frightful thoughts that cold shivers go running down my spine. Does any of you know this woman? *The three shake their heads.* How about you?

GALY GAY: I've seen many things in my life, from Ireland to Kilkoa, but I never before set eyes on this woman.

FAIRCHILD: Tell the woman your name.

GALY GAY: Jeraiah Jip.

MRS GALY GAY: This is the limit! All the same, sergeant, now I come to look at him I almost get the feeling that he is somehow different from my husband Galy Gay the porter, somehow different though I couldn't put my finger on it.

FAIRCHILD: We'll soon put our finger on it, never you mind. *He goes out with Mrs Galy Gay.*

GALY GAY *dances to the centre of the stage, singing*:

O moon of Alabama
You must go under soon!
Our dear old good old mamma
Would like a brand-new moon.

He goes up to Jesse beaming. All over Ireland the Galy Gays are famous for banging the nail home in any situation.

URIAH *to Polly*: Before the sun has set seven times this man must be another man.

POLLY: Can it really be done, Uriah? Changing one man into another?

URIAH: Yes, one man is like the other. Man equals man.

POLLY: But Uriah, the army can move off any minute, you know.

URIAH: Of course the army can move off any minute. But you can see this canteen is still here, can't you? Don't you realise that the gunners are still holding race meetings? Let me tell you that God would never agree to ruin our sort by getting the army on the move this very day. He'd certainly think twice about that.

POLLY: Listen.

Drums and bugles give the signal for departure. The three fall in and stand to attention.

FAIRCHILD *offstage, shouting*: The Army will move to the northern frontiers! Starting time zero two one zero hours tonight!

Interlude

Spoken by the Widow Leokadja Begbick.

Herr Bertolt Brecht maintains man equals man
– A view that has been around since time began.
But then Herr Brecht points out how far one can
Manoeuvre and manipulate that man.
Tonight you are going to see a man reassembled like a car
Leaving all his individual components just as they are.
He has some kind friends by whom he is pressed
Entirely in his own interest
To conform with this world and its twists and turns
And give up pursuing his own fishy concerns.
So whatever the purpose of his various transformations
He always lives up to his friends' expectations.
Indeed if we people were to let him out of our sight
They could easily make a butcher of him overnight.
Herr Bertolt Brecht hopes you'll feel the ground on
    which you stand
Slither between your toes like shifting sand
So that the case of Galy Gay the porter makes you aware
Life on this earth is a hazardous affair.

9
The Canteen

The sounds of an army breaking camp. A loud voice is heard from backstage.

THE VOICE: War has broken out as predicted. The Army will move to the northern frontier. The Queen calls on her

troops to take their guns and elephants and board the
trains, and orders those trains to head for the northern
frontier. Your General therefore commands you to be seated
in those trains before the moon is up.

Widow Begbick sits behind her bar, smoking.

BEGBICK:
> In Yehoo, the city that is always crowded and
> Where no one stays, they sing
> A song of the Flow of Things
> Which starts with:

She sings:

> Don't try to hold on to the wave
> That's breaking against your foot: so long as
> You stand in the stream fresh waves
> Will always keep breaking against it.

*She stands up, takes a stick and starts pushing back the canvas
awnings.*

> I was seven years in one place, had a roof over
> My head
> And was not alone.
> But the man who kept me fed and who was unlike anyone
>   else
> One day
> Lay unrecognisable beneath a dead man's shroud.
> All the same that evening I ate my supper
> And soon I let off the room in which we had
> Embraced one another
> And the room kept me fed
> And now that it no longer feeds me
> I continue to eat.
> I said:

Sings:

> Don't try to hold on to the wave
> That's breaking against your foot: so long as
> You stand in the stream fresh waves
> Will always keep breaking against it.

She sits down at the bar again. The three enter with several other soldiers.

URIAH *in the centre*: My friends, war has broken out. The period of disorder is over. So no more allowances can be made for private inclinations. Galy Gay, the porter from Kilkoa, has accordingly to be transformed in double quick time into the soldier Jeraiah Jip. To this end we shall get him involved in a bit of business, as is normal in our day and age, which will mean constructing an artificial elephant. Polly, take this pole and the elephant's head that's hanging on that wall, while you, Jesse, take this bottle and pour it whenever Galy Gay wants to check if the elephant can make water. And I shall spread this map over the two of you. *They build an artificial elephant.* We'll present him with this elephant and bring along a buyer, and then if he sells the elephant we'll arrest him and say: How do you come to be selling a WD elephant? At that point he will surely think it better to be Jeraiah Jip, a soldier proceeding to the northern frontier, than Galy Gay, a criminal with some chance of actually being shot.

A SOLDIER: Do you people really imagine he's going to take that thing for an elephant?

JESSE: Is it all that bad?

URIAH: He'll take it for an elephant all right, let me tell you. He'd take this beer bottle for an elephant if somebody points at it and says: I want to buy that elephant.

SOLDIER: Then you need a buyer.

URIAH *calling out*: Widow Begbick! *Begbick steps forward.* Will you play the buyer?

BEGBICK: Yes, because my beer waggon is going to get left behind unless somebody helps me to pack it up.

URIAH: Just tell the man who's about to come in that you want to buy this elephant, then we'll help pack up your canteen. And you must pay cash.

BEGBICK: Right. *She goes back to her place.*

GALY GAY *enters*: Has the elephant arrived?

URIAH: Mr Gay, your bit of business is under way. It concerns the unregistered army surplus elephant Billy Humph. The deal consists in auctioning him off unobtrusively – only to private bidders of course.

GALY GAY: That is entirely clear. Who is auctioning him off?

URIAH: Someone who signs as owner.

GALY GAY: Who is to sign as owner?

URIAH: Would you care to sign as owner, Mr Gay?

GALY GAY: Have we a buyer?

URIAH: Yes.

GALY GAY: My name, of course, must not be mentioned.

URIAH: Right. Would you care to smoke a cigar?

GALY GAY *suspiciously*: Why?

URIAH: Just to keep you from worrying, as the elephant has a slight cold.

GALY GAY: Where is the buyer?

BEGBICK *comes forward*: Oh, Mr Galy Gay, I am looking for an elephant. Would you have one, by any chance?

GALY GAY: Widow Begbick, I might have one for you.

BEGBICK: But first of all take my wall down, the gunners will soon be here.

THE SOLDIERS: Yes, Widow Begbick.

The soldiers take down one wall of the canteen. The elephant is dimly visible.

JESSE *to Begbick*: I tell you, Widow Begbick, if you take the long view what is happening here is an historic event. For what is happening here? Personality itself is being put under the microscope, we are getting under the skin of the colourful character. Steps are being taken. Technology intervenes. At the lathe or at the conveyor belt great men and little men are the same, even in stature. Personality! Remember that the ancient Assyrians, Widow Begbick, depicted personality as a tree branching out. Like this, branching out! After which, Widow Begbick, it branches in again. How does Copernicus put it? What turns? The earth turns. The earth, in other words the human race. According to Copernicus. I.e., man is not in the centre. Take a look at him, now. Is that what is supposed to stand in the centre? It's antediluvian. Man is nothing. Modern science has proved that everything is relative. What does that mean? Table, bench, water, shoehorn – all relative. You, Widow Begbick, me – relative. Look into my eyes, Widow Begbick, it's an historic moment. Man is in the centre, but only relatively speaking. *Both go off.*

No. I

URIAH *calls out*: Number One: The Elephant Deal. The MG section transfers an elephant to the man whose name must not be mentioned.

GALY GAY: One more swig from the cherry brandy bottle, one more puff at the Corona Corona, then the plunge into life.

URIAH *introduces the elephant to Galy Gay*: Billy Humph, champion of Bengal, elephant in Her Majesty's service.

GALY GAY *sees the elephant and is alarmed*: Is this the WD elephant?

A SOLDIER: He's got a bad cold, as you can see from his scarf.

GALY GAY *worried, walks round the elephant*: His scarf isn't the worst thing about him.

BEGBICK: I am the buyer. *She points to the elephant.* Sell me that elephant.

GALY GAY: Do you truly want to buy this elephant?

BEGBICK: It makes no difference how big or small he is; it's just that I've wanted to buy an elephant ever since I was a child.

GALY GAY: Is he truly what you imagined?

BEGBICK: When I was a child I wanted an elephant as big as the Hindu Kush, but today this one will do.

GALY GAY: Well, Widow Begbick, if you truly wish to buy this elephant I am the owner.

A SOLDIER *comes running from the rear*: Psst . . . psst . . . Bloody Five is going round the camp checking all railway trucks.

THE SOLDIERS: The Human Typhoon!

BEGBICK: Stay here; nobody's taking this elephant off me. *Begbick and the soldiers hurry off.*

URIAH *to Galy Gay*: Look after the elephant for a moment, will you? *Hands him the rope.*

GALY GAY: But what about me, Mr Uriah, where am I supposed to go?

URIAH: Just stay there. *He runs off after the other soldiers. Galy Gay holds the rope by the extreme end.*

GALY GAY *alone*: My mother used to say: No one knows anything for sure. But you know nothing whatsoever. This morning, Galy Gay, you went out to buy a small fish and now you have got a large elephant, and nobody knows what will happen tomorrow. It's no concern of yours so long as you get your cheque.

URIAH *looks in*: So help me, he's not even looking at the elephant. He's keeping as far from it as he can. *Fairchild is seen passing by in the background.* The Tiger of Kilkoa was just passing by.

Uriah, Begbick and the rest of the soldiers reappear.

No. II

URIAH *calls out*: And now for Number Two: the Elephant Auction. The man whose name must not be mentioned sells the elephant.

Galy Gay fetches a bell; Begbick puts a wooden bucket upside down in mid-stage.

A SOLDIER: Got any more doubts about that elephant, mate?

GALY GAY: As somebody is buying him I have no doubts.

URIAH: That's it: if somebody is buying him he must be all right.

GALY GAY: I can't say no to that. Elephant equals elephant, particularly when he is being bought.

He mounts the bucket to auction off the elephant, who is standing beside him in the centre of the group.

GALY GAY: Let's get on with the sale. I hereby invite bids for Billy Humph, the champion of Bengal. He was born, as sure as you see him standing here, in the southern Punjab. Seven Rajahs stood by his cradle. His mother was white. He is sixty-five years old. That's no great age. Thirteen hundredweight, he weighs, and a forest that has to be cleared is to him like a blade of grass in the wind. Billy Humph, as you see him now, represents a small goldmine for his eventual possessor.

URIAH: And here comes Widow Begbick with the cheque.

BEGBICK: Does this elephant belong to you?

GALY GAY: Like my own foot.

A SOLDIER: Billy must be pretty old, to judge from his uncommonly stiff deportment.

BEGBICK: So you will have to bring the price down a little.

GALY GAY: His cost was two hundred rupees ex works, and he will be worth that until he goes to his grave.

BEGBICK *examines him*: Two hundred rupees with a belly sagging like that?

GALY GAY: In my view he is nevertheless the thing for a widow.

BEGBICK: Very well. But is he in good health? *Billy Humph makes water.* That will do. I see that he is a healthy elephant. Five hundred rupees.

GALY GAY: Five hundred rupees. Going, going, gone at five hundred rupees. Widow Begbick, you will take over this elephant from me as its previous owner, and settle by cheque.

BEGBICK: Your name?

GALY GAY: Is not to be mentioned.

BEGBICK: Kindly lend me a pencil, Mr Uriah, so that I may make out a cheque to this gentleman who wishes his name not to be mentioned.

URIAH *aside to the soldiers*: Arrest him when he takes the cheque.

BEGBICK: Here is your cheque, man whose name is not to be mentioned.

GALY GAY: And here, Widow Begbick, is your elephant.

A SOLDIER *laying his hand on Galy Gay's shoulder*: In the name of the British Army, what are you up to?

GALY GAY: Me? Nothing. *He laughs foolishly.*

THE SOLDIER: What is that elephant you have got there?

GALY GAY: Which elephant do you mean?

THE SOLDIER: The one behind you, broadly speaking. No prevaricating, now.

GALY GAY: I know not the elephant.

SOLDIERS: Cor!

A SOLDIER: We can testify that this gentleman said the elephant belonged to him.

BEGBICK: He said it belonged to him like his own foot.

GALY GAY *starts to go*: Unfortunately I have to go as my wife is expecting me urgently. *He forces his way through the group.* I'll be back to discuss the matter with you. Good night. *To Billy, who is following him*: You stay here, Billy, don't be so pig-headed. That's sugar cane growing over there.

URIAH: Halt! Cover that criminal with your service pistols, yes, a criminal, that's what he is.

Polly, inside Billy Humph, laughs loudly. Uriah hits him.

URIAH: Shut up, Polly!

The front canvas slips, leaving Polly visible.

POLLY: Damnation!

Galy Gay, now utterly bewildered, looks at Polly. Then he looks from one to the other. The elephant runs away.

BEGBICK: What is going on? That's no elephant, it's just men and tarpaulin. The whole thing's phoney. Such a phoney elephant for my genuine money!

URIAH: Widow Begbick, the criminal will forthwith be bound with cords and flung into the latrine.

The soldiers bind Galy Gay and put him into a pit so that only his head is visible. The artillery is heard rolling by.

BEGBICK: The gunners are loading up. When are you lot going to pack my canteen? You know, it is not just your man that has got to be dismantled but my canteen too.

All the soldiers begin packing up the canteen. Before they have finished Uriah chases them away. Begbick comes forward with a basket loaded with dirty tarpaulins, kneels beside a small trapdoor and washes them. Galy Gay listens to her song.

> In this way I too had a name
> And those who heard that name in the city said 'It's a
>   good name'
> But one night I drank four glasses of schnapps
> And one morning I found chalked on my door
> A bad word.
> Then the milkman took back my milk again.
> My name was finished.
> Like linen that once was white and gets dirty
> And can go white once more if you wash it
> But hold it up to the light, and look: it's not
> The same linen.
> So don't speak your name so distinctly. What is the point?

Considering that you are always using it to name a differ-
ent person.
And wherefore such loud opinions, forget them.
What were they, did you say? Never remember
Anything longer than its own duration.

She sings:

Don't try to hold on to the wave
That's breaking against your foot: so long as
You stand in the stream fresh waves
Will always keep breaking against it.

She goes off. Uriah and the soldiers come in from the rear.

No. III

URIAH *calls out*: And now comes Number Three: the Trial
of the Man Whose Name is Not to be Mentioned. Form a
circle round the criminal and interrogate him and do not
stop until you know the naked truth.

GALY GAY: May I have permission to say something?

URIAH: You have said a lot tonight, mister. Does anyone
know what the man was called who put the elephant up for
auction?

A SOLDIER: He was called Galy Gay.

URIAH: Can anyone testify to that?

THE SOLDIERS: We can testify to that.

URIAH: What has the accused got to say on that point?

GALY GAY: He was someone whose name was not to be mentioned.

The soldiers grumble.

A SOLDIER: I heard him say he was Galy Gay.

URIAH: Isn't that you?

GALY GAY *slyly*: Well, supposing I were Galy Gay, perhaps I might be the man you are looking for.

URIAH: Then you are not Galy Gay?

GALY GAY *under his breath*: No, I am not.

URIAH: And perhaps you were not even present when Billy Humph was put up for auction?

GALY GAY: No, I was not present.

URIAH: But you saw that it was someone called Galy Gay who conducted the sale?

GALY GAY: Yes, I can testify to that.

URIAH: So now you are saying that you were present after all?

GALY GAY: I can testify to that.

URIAH: Did you all hear? Do you see the moon? The moon has risen, and here he is up to his neck in this crooked elephant business. As for Billy Humph, wasn't there something a bit wrong with him?

JESSE: There certainly was.

A SOLDIER: The man called it an elephant, but it was nothing of the sort, just made of paper.

URIAH: In other words he was selling a phoney elephant. Which of course carries the death penalty. What have you to say to that?

GALY GAY: Perhaps another elephant might not have taken him for an elephant. It is very hard to keep all this straight, your Honour.

URIAH: Indeed it is extremely complicated, but I think you will have to be shot none the less, because your behaviour has been highly suspicious. *Galy Gay is silent.* Come to think of it, I have heard of a soldier by the name of Jip who even answered to that name at sundry roll calls, while trying to make people think his name was Galy Gay. Are you by any chance the Jip in question?

GALY GAY: No, certainly not.

URIAH: So you are not called Jip? Then what is your name? No answer? Then you are a man whose name is not to be mentioned. Are you by any chance the man at the elephant auction whose name was not to be mentioned? What? Again no answer? That is immensely suspicious, almost enough to get you convicted. What is more, the criminal who sold the elephant is said to have been a man with a moustache, and you have got a moustache. Come on, men, all this calls for discussion. *He goes to the rear with the soldiers. Two of them stay with Galy Gay.*

URIAH *as he leaves*: Now he doesn't want to be Galy Gay any more.

GALY GAY *after a pause*: Can you two hear what they are saying?

A SOLDIER: No.

GALY GAY: Are they saying that I am this Galy Gay?

SECOND SOLDIER: They are saying it's no longer all that certain.

GALY GAY: Better remember: one man equals no man.

SECOND SOLDIER: Anybody know who this war's against?

FIRST SOLDIER: If they need cotton it'll be Tibet, and if they need wool it'll be Pamir.

JESSE *arriving*: Surely that's Galy Gay sitting tied up here?

FIRST SOLDIER: Hey, you, answer him.

GALY GAY: I think you're mistaking me for someone else, Jesse. Take a good look at me.

JESSE: Ha, aren't you Galy Gay? *Galy Gay shakes his head.* Leave us for a moment; he has just been sentenced to death, so I have to speak to him.
The two soldiers go to the rear.

GALY GAY: Has it come to that? Oh, Jesse, help me, you are a great soldier.

JESSE: How did it happen?

GALY GAY: Well, Jesse, it's like this: I don't know. There we were, smoking and drinking, and I talked my soul away.

JESSE: I heard them say it's someone called Galy Gay who's supposed to be killed.

GALY GAY: Out of the question.

JESSE: Ha, aren't you Galy Gay?

GALY GAY: Wipe the sweat from my face, Jesse.

JESSE *does so*: Look me straight in the eye, I'm your friend Jesse. Aren't you Galy Gay from Kilkoa?

GALY GAY: No, you must have got it wrong.

JESSE: There were four of us when we left Kankerdan. Were you with us then?

GALY GAY: Yes, at Kankerdan I was with you.

JESSE *goes to the rear to the other soldiers*: The moon is not yet up, and he is already wanting to be Jip.

URIAH: All the same, I think we'd better put a little more fear of death into him.

The artillery is heard rolling by.

BEGBICK *enters*: That's the gunners, Uriah. Help me fold up the awnings. And the rest of you, carry on taking it down. *The soldiers go on loading sections of the canteen into the waggon. Just one plank wall remains standing. Uriah and Begbick fold the tarpaulins.*

I spoke to many people and listened
Carefully and heard many opinions
And heard many say of many things: 'That is for sure'.
But when they came back they spoke differently from the
    way they spoke earlier
And it was something else of which they said: 'That is for
    sure'.
At that I told myself: of all sure things
The surest is doubt.

Uriah goes to the rear. So does Begbick with her laundry basket, passing Galy Gay. She sings:

Don't try to hold on to the wave
That's breaking against your foot: so long as
You stand in the stream fresh waves
Will always keep breaking against it.

GALY GAY: Widow Begbick, may I ask you to get a pair of scissors and cut my moustache off?

BEGBICK: What for?

GALY GAY: I know what for all right.

Begbick cuts off his moustache, wraps it in a cloth and takes it to the waggon. The soldiers reappear.

No. IV

URIAH *calls out*: And now for Number Four: the Execution of Galy Gay in the military cantoment at Kilkoa.

BEGBICK *comes up to him*: Mr Uriah, I have something for you here. *She whispers something in his ear and gives him the cloth with the moustache in it.*

URIAH *goes to the latrine pit where Galy Gay is*: Has the accused man anything further to say?

GALY GAY: Your Honour, they tell me the criminal who sold the elephant was a man with a moustache, and I have no moustache.

URIAH *silently showing him the open cloth with the moustache*: And what is this? You've really convicted yourself this time, my man, because cutting off that moustache of yours just shows your guilty conscience. Come now, man without a name, and hear the verdict of the Kilkoa court-martial which says that you are to be shot by a firing squad of five. *The soldiers drag Galy Gay out of the latrine pit.*

GALY GAY *shouting*: You can't do that to me.

URIAH: You'll find that we can, though. Listen carefully, my man: first because you stole and sold a WD elephant – which is theft –, secondly because you sold an elephant which was no elephant – which is fraud –, and thirdly because you are unable to produce any kind of name or identity document and may well be a spy – which is high treason.

GALY GAY: Oh, Uriah, why are you treating me like this?

URIAH: Come along now and conduct yourself as a good
soldier like the army taught you. Quick march! Get moving
so they can shoot you.

GALY GAY: Oh, do not be so hasty. I am not the man you are
looking for. I have never met him. My name is Jip, I can
swear it is. What is an elephant compared to a man's life?
I didn't see that elephant, it was just a rope I was holding.
Don't go away, please. I'm someone quite different. I am
not Galy Gay. I am not.

JESSE: Oh yes you are, and nobody else. Under the three
rubber trees of Kilkoa Galy Gay will see his blood flowing.
Get moving, Galy Gay.

GALY GAY: O God! Wait a minute, there has to be an official
record listing the charges and showing that I didn't do it
and that my name is not Galy Gay. Every detail must be
weighed. You can't rush this sort of thing when a man is
about to be slaughtered.

JESSE: Quick march!

GALY GAY: What do you mean, quick march? I am not the
man you're looking for. All I wanted was to buy a fish, but
where do you find fish around here? What are those guns
rolling by? What is that battle music blaring away? No, I
am not budging. I'll cling to the grass. The whole thing
must stop. And why is no one here when a man is being
slaughtered?

BEGBICK: Once they start loading the elephants if you lot
aren't ready you can be written off. *She goes off.*
*Galy Gay is led back and forth; he strides like the protagonist in
a tragedy.*

JESSE: Make way for the criminal whom the court martial
has condemned to death.

SOLDIERS: Look, there's someone who's going to be shot.
Perhaps it's a pity, he's not old yet. – And he doesn't know
how he got into this.

URIAH: Halt! Would you like to relieve yourself one last time?

GALY GAY: Yes.

URIAH: Guard him closely.

GALY GAY: They say that once the elephants arrive the soldiers will have to leave, so I must take my time to allow the elephants to get here.

SOLDIERS: Hurry up!

GALY GAY: I can't. Is that the moon?

SOLDIERS: Yes. – It's getting late.

GALY GAY: Isn't that the Widow Begbick's bar where we always used to drink?

URIAH: No, my boy. This is the rifle range and here is the 'Johnny don't wet yourself' wall. Hey! Get fell in over there, you lot! And load your rifles. There should be five of them.

SOLDIERS: It's so hard to see in this light.

URIAH: Yes, it is very hard.

GALY GAY: Wait a moment, this won't do. You people must be able to see when you shoot.

URIAH *to Jesse*: Take that paper lantern and hold it beside him. *He blindfolds Galy Gay. In a loud voice*: Load your rifles! *Under his breath*: What are you doing, Polly? That's a live round you're putting in. Take it out.

POLLY: So sorry, I almost really loaded. And that could almost have led to a real disaster.

The elephants are heard passing in the background. The soldiers stand for a moment as if transfixed.

BEGBICK *off, calls*: The elephants!

URIAH: It's all no use. He has got to be shot. I'll count up to three. One!

GALY GAY: All right, Uriah, enough is enough. The elephants have arrived, haven't they? Am I supposed to go on standing here, Uriah? But why are you all keeping so horribly still?

URIAH: Two!

GALY GAY *laughing*: You're a queer cuss, Uriah. I can't see you, because you blindfolded me. But your voice sounds just like if you were dead serious about it.

URIAH: And one more makes . . .

GALY GAY: Whoah, don't say three, or you'll regret it. If you shoot now you're bound to hit me. Whoah! No, not yet. Listen to me. I confess! I confess I don't know what has been happening to me. Believe me, and don't laugh: I'm a man who doesn't know who he is. But I am not Galy Gay, that much I do know. I'm not the man who is supposed to be shot. Who am I, though? Because I've forgotten. Last night when it rained I still knew. It did rain last night, didn't it? I beseech you, when you look over here or where this voice is coming from, it's me, I beseech you. Call up that place, say Galy Gay or something to it, be merciful, give me a bit of meat. Where it goes in will be Galy Gay, and likewise where it comes out. Or at the very least if you come across a man who has forgotten who he is, that'll be me. And it's him I am beseeching you to let go.

Uriah has whispered something in Polly's ear; then Polly runs up behind Galy Gay and raises a big club over his head

URIAH: Once equals never! Three!

Galy Gay lets out a scream.

URIAH: Fire!

Galy Gay falls down in a faint.

POLLY: Whoah! He fell of his own accord.

URIAH *shouts*: Fire! So that he can hear he's dead.

The soldiers fire into the air.

URIAH: Leave him there and get ready to move off.

Galy Gay is left lying as all the others exeunt.

No. IVa

Begbick and the three are sitting outside the packed waggon at a table with five chairs. To one side lies Galy Gay covered with a sack.

JESSE: Here's the sergeant coming. Can you stop him poking his nose into our business, Widow Begbick?

Fairchild is seen approaching in civilian clothes.

BEGBICK: Yes, because that is a civilian coming. *To Fairchild, who is standing in the doorway*: Come and join us, Charles.

FAIRCHILD: There you sit, you Gomorrah! *Standing over Galy Gay*: And what is this sozzled carcass? *Silence. He pounds on the table.* Atten – shun!

URIAH *from behind knocks his hat down over his ears*: Stop your gob, civvy!
Laughter.

FAIRCHILD: Go ahead, mutiny, you sons of a gun! Observe my suit and laugh! Tear up my name that is famous from Calcutta to Cooch Behar! Give me a drink and then I'll shoot you!

URIAH: Come on, Fairchild old boy, show us what a brilliant shot you are.

FAIRCHILD: No.

BEGBICK: Nine women out of every ten fall for these top-class riflemen.

POLLY: Get cracking, Fairchild.

BEGBICK: You really should, for my sake.

FAIRCHILD: O thou Babylon! Here I place one egg – here. How many paces shall I make it?

POLLY: Four.

FAIRCHILD *takes ten paces, which Begbick counts aloud*: Here I have one perfectly ordinary service revolver. *He fires.*

JESSE *goes over to the egg*: The egg is untouched.

POLLY: Utterly.

URIAH: If anything it's got bigger.

FAIRCHILD: Strange. I thought I could hit it.
Loud laughter.

FAIRCHILD: Give me a drink. *He drinks.* I shall squash you all like bedbugs as sure as my name is Bloody Five.

URIAH: How did you actually come by the name Bloody Five?

JESSE *seated again*: Give us a demonstration.

FAIRCHILD: Shall I tell the story, Mrs Begbick?

BEGBICK: Eight women out of every nine would find this gory man divine.

FAIRCHILD: Right: here we have the River Chadze. There stand five Hindus. Hands tied behind their backs. Then along comes me with an ordinary service revolver, waves it in their faces a bit and says: this revolver has been misfiring. It has got to be tested. Like this. Then I fire – bang! down you go, that man there! – and so on four times more. That's all there was to it, gentlemen. *He sits down.*

JESSE: So that is how you came by your great name, which has made this widow your slave for life? From a human point of view, of course, one might regard your conduct as unbecoming and say you are simply a swine.

BEGBICK: Are you a monster?

FAIRCHILD: I would be very sorry if you took it like that. Your opinion means a lot to me.

BEGBICK: But do you accept it as final?

FAIRCHILD *looking deeply into her eyes*: Absolutely.

BEGBICK: In that case, my dear man, my opinion is that I must get my canteen packed up and have no more time for private matters, for now I can hear the lancers trotting past as they take their horses to be loaded.

The lancers are heard riding by.

POLLY: Are you still insisting on your own selfish desires, sir, even though the lancers are loading their horses and you have been told that for military reasons this canteen has to be packed up?

FAIRCHILD *bellowing*: Yes, I am. Give me a drink.

POLLY: All right, but we'll soon settle your hash, my boy.

JESSE: Sir, not all that far from here a man clad in British Army service dress is lying under a rough tarpaulin. He is recuperating after a hard day's work. A mere twenty-four hours ago he was still – from a military point of view – a babe in arms. His wife's voice frightened him. Without guidance he was incapable of buying a fish. In return for a cigar he was prepared to forget his father's name. Some

people took him in hand, because they happened to know
of a place for him. Since then, admittedly at the cost of
painful trials, he has become a man who will play his part
in the battles to come. You on the other hand have declined
into a mere civilian. At a time when the army is off to
restore order on the northern frontier, a move that demands beer, you big shitheap are deliberately hindering
the proprietress of an army canteen from getting her beer
waggon entrained.

POLLY: How can you hope to check our names at the last
roll-call and enter all four of them in your sergeant's note-
book as per regulations?

URIAH: How can you possibly hope to face a company thirsting to confront its countless enemies given the state you're
in? Get up!

Fairchild rises unsteadily.

POLLY: Call that getting up?

He gives Fairchild a kick in the bottom, which makes him fall down.

URIAH: Is this what they used to call the Human Typhoon?
Chuck that wreck into the bushes or he'll demoralise the
company.

The three start dragging Fairchild to the rear.

A SOLDIER *rushes in and stops at the rear*: Is Sergeant Charles
Fairchild here? The General says he is to hurry up and get
his company fallen in at the goods station.

FAIRCHILD: Don't tell him it's me.

JESSE: There is no such sergeant here.

No. V

*Begbick and the three contemplate Galy Gay, who is still lying under
the sack.*

URIAH: Widow Begbick, we have reached the end of our
assemblage. We believe that our man has now been recon-
structed.

POLLY: I'd say all he needs now is a human voice.

JESSE: Have you got a human voice for this kind of eventuality, Widow Begbick?

BEGBICK: Yes, and something for him to eat. Take this crate here and write 'Galy Gay' on it in black chalk and then put a cross. *They do so.* Then form a funeral procession and bury him. The whole operation must not last more than nine minutes, as it's already a minute past two.

URIAH *calls out*: Number Five: Obsequies and Interment of Galy Gay, last of the personalities, in the year nineteen hundred and twenty-five. *The soldiers enter, doing up their packs.* Pick up that crate there and form a neat funeral procession. *The soldiers form up at the rear with the crate.*

JESSE: And I shall step up to him and say: You are to deliver a funeral oration for Galy Gay. *To Begbick*: He won't eat anything.

BEGBICK: That kind eats even when he's nobody.
She takes her basket over to Galy Gay, removes his sack and gives him food.

GALY GAY: More!
She gives him more; then she signals to Uriah and the procession comes downstage.

GALY GAY: Who's that they're carrying?

BEGBICK That is someone who was shot at the last minute.

GALY GAY: What is he called?

BEGBICK: Wait a moment. Unless I am mistaken he was called Galy Gay.

GALY GAY: And what's to happen to him now?

BEGBICK: To whom?

GALY GAY: To this Galy Gay fellow.

BEGBICK: Now they're going to bury him.

GALY GAY: Was he a good man or a bad one?

BEGBICK: Oh, he was a dangerous man.

GALY GAY: Yes, he was shot, wasn't he; I was present.
The procession passes. Jesse stops and speaks to Galy Gay.

JESSE: Surely that is Jip? Jip, you must get up at once and

give the address at this fellow Galy Gay's funeral, as you probably knew him better than any of us.

GALY GAY: Hey, are you actually able to see me down here? *Jesse points at him.* Yes, that's right. And what am I doing now? *He bends his arm.*

JESSE: Bending your arm.

GALY GAY: So I've bent my arm twice now. And now?

JESSE: Now you are walking like a soldier.

GALY GAY: Do you people walk the same way?

JESSE: Exactly the same way.

GALY GAY: And how will you address me when you want something?

JESSE: Jip.

GALY GAY: Try saying: Jip, walk around.

JESSE: Jip, walk around. Walk around under the rubber trees and rehearse your funeral oration for Galy Gay.

GALY GAY *slowly walks over to the crate*: Is this the crate he's in?

He walks around the procession as they hold up the crate. He walks faster and faster and tries to run away. Begbick holds him back.

BEGBICK: Are you looking for something? The Army's one remedy for all diseases, up to and including cholera, is castor oil. No soldier has any disease that castor oil won't cure. Would you like some castor oil?

GALY GAY *shakes his head*:

My mother on her calendar marked the day
When I came out, and the thing that cried was me.
This bundle of flesh, nails and hair
Is me, is me.

JESSE: Yes, Jeraiah Jip, Jeraiah Jip from Tipperary.

GALY GAY: Someone who carried cucumbers for tips. Swindled by an elephant, he had to sleep quickly on a wooden chair for lack of time, because the fish water was boiling in his hut. Nor had the machine-gun yet been cleaned, for they presented him with a cigar and five rifle barrels of which one was missing. Oh, what was his name?

URIAH: Jip. Jeraiah Jip.

Sounds of train whistling.

SOLDIERS: The trains are whistling. – Now it's every man for himself. *They fling down the crate and run off.*

JESSE: The convoy leaves in six minutes. He'll have to come as he is.

URIAH: Listen, Polly, and you too, Jesse. Fellow-soldiers! We are three survivors, and now that they have started sawing through the hair by which the three of us are suspended over the precipice you had better listen carefully to what I say beneath the last wall of Kilkoa at approximately two o'clock in the morning. The man we want must be allowed a little time, since it is for all eternity that he will be changing. Therefore I, Uriah Shelley, am now drawing my service revolver and threatening you with instant death if any of you moves.

POLLY: But if he looks inside the crate we are sunk.

Galy Gay sits down beside the crate.

GALY GAY:

I could not, without instant death
Gaze into a crate at a drained face
Of some person once familiar to me from the water's surface
Into which a man looked who, so I realise, died.
Therefore I am unable to open this crate
Because this fear is in the both of me, for perhaps
I am the Both which has just come about
On our earth's transformable top surface:
A chopped-off batlike thing hanging
Betwixt rubber trees and hut, a night bird
A thing that would gladly be cheerful.
One man equals no man. Some one has to call him.

Therefore
I would gladly have looked into this chest
As the heart clings to its parents.

Given a forest, which would still be there
If no one walked through it, and the very man
Who walked through where a forest once was:
How do they recognise one another?
When he sees his own footprints among the reeds
With water spurting into them, does that puddle mean any-
    thing to him?
What is your opinion?

By what sign does Galy Gay know himself
To be Galy Gay?
Suppose his arm was cut off
And he found it in the chink of a wall
Would Galy Gay's eye know Galy Gay's arm
And Galy Gay's foot cry out: This is the one!?
Therefore I am not looking into this chest.
Moreover in my opinion the difference
Between yes and no is not all that great.
And if Galy Gay were not Galy Gay
Then he would be the drinking son of some mother who
Would be some other man's mother if she
Were not his, and thus would anyway drink.
And would have been produced in March, not in Septem-
    ber
Unless instead of March he had
Been produced only in September of this year, or already
In September the year before
Which represents that one small year's difference
That turns one man into another man.
And I, the one I and the other I
Are used and accordingly usable.
And since I never gazed at that elephant

I shall close an eye to what concerns myself
And shed what is not likeable about me and thereby
Be pleasant.

Noise of moving trains.

GALY GAY: And what trains are those? Where are they off to?
BEGBICK: This army is heading straight into the fire-belching cannon of the battles that have been planned for the
  north. Tonight a hundred thousand will march in a single
  direction. That direction is from south to north. When a
  man gets caught up in such a stream he seeks out two to
  march beside him, one right and one left. He looks for a
  rifle and a haversack and an identity disc to go round his
  neck and a number on that identity disc so that when they
  find him they can tell what unit he belonged to, so he can
  be given his place in a mass grave. Have you got an identity
  disc?
GALY GAY: Yes.
BEGBICK: What's on it?
GALY GAY: Jeraiah Jip.
BEGBICK: Well, Jeraiah Jip, better have a wash, for you look
  like a rubbish heap. Make yourself ready. The army is leaving for the northern frontier. The fire-belching cannon
  of the northern battlefields are awaiting it. The army is
  thirsting to restore order in the populous cities of the
  north.
GALY GAY *washing*: Who is the enemy?
BEGBICK: Up to now it has not been announced which
  country we are making war on. But it begins to look more
  and more like Tibet.
GALY GAY: You know something, Widow Begbick: One
  man equals no man, until some one calls him.
  The soldiers march in with their packs.
SOLDIERS: Everyone on board! – Get entrained! – Are you
  all present and correct?

URIAH: In one moment. Your funeral oration, Comrade Jip, your funeral oration!

GALY GAY *goes to the coffin*: Therefore raise up Widow Beg-bick's crate which contains this mysterious corpse, lifting it two feet high and plunging it six feet deep in the Kilkoa soil here, and listen to his funeral oration rendered by Jeraiah Jip from Tipperary, a very difficult job as I am unprepared. But never mind: here lies Galy Gay, a man who was shot. He set out to buy a small fish one morning, had acquired a large elephant by that evening and was shot in the course of the same night. Do not imagine, dearly beloved brethren, that he was of no consequence during his lifetime. Indeed he owned a straw hut on the fringes of the town as well as various other things which had best be passed over in silence. It was no great crime that he committed, good man that he was. And they can say what they like, and it was really an oversight, and I was much too drunk, gentlemen, but Man equals Man and that is why they had to shoot him. And now the wind is perceptibly cooler as it always is before dawn, and I think we should get away from here, it's an uneasy place in other ways too. *He steps away from the coffin;* But why have you people got all your kit?

POLLY: You see, this morning we are to board the waggons going to the northern frontier.

GALY GAY: Well, why haven't I got all my kit?

JESSE: Well, why hasn't he got all his kit?

Soldiers bring his equipment.

JESSE: Here's your stuff, captain.

Some soldiers carry a large bundle wrapped in straw mats to the train.

URIAH: He took his time, the swine. But we'll get him yet. *Pointing to the bundle:* That was the Human Typhoon. *All go off.*

10

In the Moving Train

Just before dawn. The company are asleep in their hammocks. Jesse, Uriah and Polly are sitting up on guard. Galy Gay is sleeping.

JESSE: The world is dreadful. Men cannot be relied on.

POLLY: The vilest and weakest thing alive is man.

JESSE: Through dust and water we have footed it down every road in this oversized country from the mountains of the Hindu Kush to the great plains of the southern Punjab; yet from Benares to Calcutta, by sun and moon, we have seen nothing but treachery. This man whom we took under our wing and who has swiped our blankets and ruined our night's sleep is like a leaky oil can. Yes and no are the same to him, he says one thing today another tomorrow. Ah, Uriah, we have tried and failed. Let us go to Leokadja Begbick, who is sitting up with the sergeant to save him from falling off his bunk, and ask her to lie down with this man so that he feels good and asks no questions. Old as she is there is still warmth in her, and once a man is lying with a woman he knows all the answers. Get up, Polly.

They go over to Widow Begbick.

JESSE: Come in, Widow Begbick, we are at a loss what to do, and are frightened of falling asleep, and here we are with this man who is ill. So you lie down with him, pretend he's spent the night with you, and make him feel good.

BEGBICK *enters half asleep*: I'll do it for seven weeks' pay.

URIAH: You shall have all we earn for seven weeks.

Begbick lies down with Galy Gay. Jesse covers them with papers.

GALY GAY *waking up*: What is it that's shaking so?

URIAH *to the others*: That is the elephant nibbling at your hut, you sniveller.

GALY GAY: What is it that's hissing so?

URIAH *to the others*: That is the fish boiling in the water, you pleasant man.

GALY GAY *gets up with difficulty and looks out of the window*: A woman, sleeping bags. Telegraph poles. It's a train.

JESSE: Pretend you are all asleep.

The three pretend to be asleep.

GALY GAY *goes up to a sleeping bag*: Hey, you.

SOLDIER: What do you want?

GALY GAY: Where are you people going?

SOLDIER *opening one eye*: To the front. *Goes back to sleep.*

GALY GAY: These are soldiers. *Looks out of the window again, then wakes another.* Mr Soldier, what is the time? *No answer.* Almost morning. What day of the week is it?

SOLDIER: Between Thursday and Friday.

GALY GAY: I must get off. Hey, you, the train must be stopped.

SOLDIER: This train doesn't stop.

GALY GAY: If this train doesn't stop and everyone's sleeping I'd better lie down too and sleep till it does stop. *Sees Widow Begbick.* There's a woman lying beside me. Who is this woman who lay beside me in the night?

JESSE: Hullo, mate, good morning.

GALY GAY: Oh, I'm so glad to see you, Mr Jesse.

JESSE: Aren't you living it up? Lying there with a woman beside you and letting everybody see.

GALY GAY: Isn't it remarkable? Positively indecent, eh? But a man is a man, you know. He is not always master of himself. For instance, here am I waking up, and there's a woman lying beside me.

JESSE: Why, so there is.

GALY GAY: And would you believe that there are times when I don't know a woman who is lying beside me like this in the morning? To be perfectly frank and speaking as man to man, I don't know this woman. And, Mr Jesse, as one man to another, would you be able to tell me who she is?

JESSE: Oh you line-shooter! This time of course it's Widow

Leokadja Begbick. Duck your head in a pail of water and you'll know your lady friend all right. I don't suppose you know your own name, then, either?

GALY GAY: I do.

JESSE: All right, what is your name?

GALY GAY *is silent*.

JESSE: So you know your name?

GALY GAY: Yes.

JESSE: That's good. A man needs to know who he is when he is off to the war.

GALY GAY: Is there a war?

JESSE: Yes, the Tibetan War.

GALY GAY: The Tibetan. But suppose just for the moment a man didn't know who he is, that would be funny when he is off to the war, wouldn't it? Now you mentioned Tibet, sir, that's a place I always wanted to see. I used to know a man had a wife came from the province of Sikkim, which is on the Tibetan frontier. They are good people there, she used to say.

BEGBICK: Jippie, where are you?

GALY GAY: Who is she talking to?

JESSE: I think she is talking to you.

GALY GAY: Here.

BEGBICK: Come and give us a kiss, Jippie.

GALY GAY: I don't mind if I do, but I think you have got me a bit muddled with someone else.

BEGBICK: Jippie!

JESSE: This gentleman claims his head is not quite clear; he says he doesn't know you.

BEGBICK: Oh, how can you humiliate me so in front of this gentleman?

GALY GAY: If I duck my head in this pail of water I'll know you right away. *He sticks his head into the pail of water.*

BEGBICK: Do you know me now?

GALY GAY *lying*: Yes.

POLLY: Then you also know who you yourself are?

GALY GAY *slyly*: Didn't I know that?

POLLY: No, because you were out of your mind and claimed to be someone else.

GALY GAY: Who was I, then?

JESSE: You're not getting much better, I see. What's more I still think you are a public menace, because last night when we called you by your right name you turned as dangerous as any murderer.

GALY GAY: All I know is that my name is Galy Gay.

JESSE: Listen to that, you people, he's starting all over again. You'd better call him Galy Gay like he says, or he'll throw another fit.

URIAH: Oh bollocks. Mr Jip from Ireland, consider yourself free to play the wild man right up to the point where you get tied to a post outside the canteen and the night rain comes down. We who have been your mates since the battle of the River Chadze would sell our shirts to make things easier for you.

GALY GAY: No need for that about the shirts.

URIAH: Call him anything he wants.

JESSE: Shut up, Uriah. Would you care for a glass of water, Galy Gay?

GALY GAY: Yes, that is my name.

JESSE: Of course, Galy Gay. How could you be called anything else? Just take it easy, lie down. Tomorrow they will put you in hospital, in a nice comfortable bed with plenty of castor oil, and that will relieve you, Galy Gay. Tread delicately, all of you, our friend Jip, I mean Galy Gay, is unwell.

GALY GAY: Let me tell you, gentlemen, the situation is beyond me. But when it is a matter of carrying a cabin trunk, never mind how heavy it is, they say every cabin trunk is supposed to have its soft spot.

POLLY *ostensibly aside to Jesse*: Just keep him away from that pouch around his neck, or he'll read his real name in his paybook and throw another fit.

JESSE: Oh, how good a paybook is! How easily one forgets things! Therefore we soldiers, being unable to carry everything at once in our heads, have a pouch on a cord round each man's neck containing a paybook with his name in it. Because if a man spends too much time thinking about his name it is not good.

GALY GAY *goes to the rear, looks gloomily at his paybook and returns to his corner.* In future I shall give up thinking. I shall just sit on my bottom and count the telegraph poles.

THE VOICE OF SERGEANT FAIRCHILD: O misery, o awakening! Where is my name that was famous from Calcutta to Couch Behar? Even the uniform I wore is gone. They bundled me into a train like a calf going to the slaughterhouse. They stopped my mouth with a civilitic hat and the whole train knows that I am no longer Bloody Five. I will go and fix this train so that it can be tossed on to a rubbish dump like a twisted stovepipe. That is plain as a pikestaff.

JESSE: Bloody Five! Wake up, Widow Begbick!
Fairchild enters in soiled civilian clothes.

GALY GAY: Have you been having trouble with your name?

FAIRCHILD: You are the most melancholy specimen of them all, and I shall start by crushing you. Tonight I am going to chop you all up ready for the cannery. *He sees the Widow Begbick sitting there; she smiles.* I'll be damned! There you are still, you Gomorrah! What have you done to me that I am no longer Bloody Five? Get away from me! *Begbick laughs.* What are these clothes I'm wearing? Do you call them suitable? And what is this head I've got? Do you suppose that's pleasant? Am I to lie down with you again, you Sodom?

BEGBICK: If you want to, do.

FAIRCHILD: I do not want to! Get away from me! The eyes of this country are upon me. I used to be a big gun. My name is Bloody Five. The pages of the history books are criss-crossed with that name, in triplicate.

BEGBICK: Then don't if you don't want to.

FAIRCHILD: Don't you realise that my manhood makes me weak when you sit there like that?

BEGBICK: Then pluck out your manhood, my boy.

FAIRCHILD: No need to tell me twice. *He goes out.*

GALY GAY *cries out after him*: Stop! Don't take any steps on account of your name! A name is an uncertain thing, you can't build on it.

FAIRCHILD: That is plain as a pikestaff. That is the answer. There we have a rope. There we have a service pistol. That's where we draw the line. Mutineers will be shot. That is plain as a pikestaff. 'Johnny Bowlegs, pack your kit.' No girl in this world will ever cost me a penny again. That is plain as a pikestaff. And I shall remain cool as a cucumber. I accept full responsibility. I have to do it if I am to go on being Bloody Five.

A shot is heard.

GALY GAY *who has been standing in the doorway for some time laughs*. Fire!

SOLDIERS *in the waggons on either side*: Did you hear that scream? – Who was screaming? – Somebody must have got hurt. They've all stopped singing, even up at the front of the train. – Listen.

GALY GAY: I know who screamed and I know why. On account of his name this gentleman has done something extremely bloody to himself. He has shot off his manhood. Witnessing that was a great stroke of luck for me. Now I realise where such stubbornness gets you and what a bloody thing it is when a man is never satisfied with himself and makes so much fuss about his name. *He runs over to Widow Begbick.* Don't get the idea that I don't know you. I know you very well indeed. And anyway it doesn't matter. But tell me quickly, how far away is the town where we met?

BEGBICK: Many days' march, and it gets further every minute.

GALY GAY: How many days' march?

BEGBICK: At the instant when you asked it was at least a hundred days' march.

GALY GAY: And how many men are there here travelling to Tibet?

BEGBICK: A hundred thousand. One equals no one.

GALY GAY: Of course. A hundred thousand. And what do they eat?

BEGBICK: Dried fish and rice.

GALY GAY: Everybody the same?

BEGBICK: Everybody the same.

GALY GAY: Of course. Everybody the same.

BEGBICK: They all have hammocks to sleep in, each man his own, and denims for summer.

GALY GAY: And in the winter?

BEGBICK: Khaki in winter.

GALY GAY: And women?

BEGBICK: The same.

GALY GAY: Women the same.

BEGBICK: And now, do you also know who you are?

GALY GAY: Jeraiah Jip, that's my name. *He runs over to the three others and shows them his name in his paybook.*

JESSE *and the others smile*: Right. You know how to keep putting your name across, don't you, comrade Jip?

GALY GAY: How about food?

Polly brings him a dish of rice.

GALY GAY: Yes, it is most important that I eat. *Eats.* How many days' march did you say this train covers in one minute?

BEGBICK: Ten.

POLLY: Just look how he's making himself at home. How he stares at everything and counts the telegraph poles and gloats at the speed we are going.

JESSE: I cannot bear the sight of him. It is truly loathsome when a mammoth, just because a couple of rifles are shoved under his nose, chooses to turn into a louse rather than be decently gathered to the bosom of his forebears.

URIAH: On the contrary, it's a sign of vitality. So long as Jip doesn't come after us now singing 'For man equals man, since time began' I think we will be over the hump.

A SOLDIER: What's that noise in the air?

URIAH *with a nasty smile*: That is the roaring of the artillery, for we are nearing the hills of Tibet.

GALY GAY: Isn't there some more rice?

11

Deep in Remote Tibet Lies the Mountain Fortress of Sir El-Djowr

And on a hilltop Jeraiah Jip sits waiting amid the thunder of guns

VOICES FROM BELOW: This is as far as we can go. – This is the fortress of Sir El-Djowr which blocks the pass into Tibet.

GALY GAY'S VOICE *behind the hill*: At the double! Or we'll be too late. *He appears, carrying a gun tripod on his shoulder.* Out of the train and straight into battle. That's what I like. A gun takes some living up to.

JIP: Haven't you seen a machine-gun section with only three men in it?

GALY GAY *charging on irresistibly like a war elephant*: There's no such thing, soldier. Our section consists of four men, for instance. One man to the right of you, one to the left and one behind you, after which it's proper for it to get through any pass.

BEGBICK *appears, carrying a gun barrel on her back*: Don't run so fast, Jippie. The trouble is, you've got a heart like a lion. *The three soldiers appear, groaning as they drag their machine-gun.*

JIP: Hullo, Uriah, hullo, Jesse, hullo, Polly! Here I am again. *The three soldiers pretend not to see him.*

JESSE: We must get this machine-gun set up at once.

URIAH: The gunfire's so noisy already you can't hear yourself speak.

POLLY: We must keep a particularly sharp eye on the fortress of Sir El-Djowr.

GALY GAY: And I want to have first shot. Something is holding us up, it must be taken out. All these gentlemen here can't be kept waiting. It won't hurt the mountain. Jesse, Uriah, Polly! The battle is starting, and I already feel the urge to sink my teeth in the enemy's throat. *And he and Widow Begbick together assemble the gun.*

JIP: Hullo, Jesse, hullo, Uriah, hullo, Polly! How are you all? Long time no see. I was a bit held up, you know. I hope you haven't had any trouble on my account. I couldn't make it sooner. I'm really glad to be back. But why don't you say something?

POLLY: How can we be of service to you, sir? *Polly puts a dish of rice on the gun for Galy Gay.* Won't you eat your rice ration? The battle will be starting soon.

GALY GAY: Gimme! *He eats.* Yes: first I eat my rice ration, then I get my correct apportionment of whisky, and while I am eating and drinking I can study this mountain fortress and try to find its soft spot. After that it will be a piece of cake.

JIP: Your voice has completely changed, Polly, but you still like to have your joke. Me, I was employed in a flourishing business, but I had to leave. For your sakes, of course. You aren't angry, are you?

URIAH: This is where I fear we must inform you that you seem to have come to the wrong address.

POLLY: We don't even know you.

JESSE: It is of course possible that we have met somewhere. But the army has vast reserves of manpower, sir.

GALY GAY: I should like another rice ration. You have not handed your ration over yet, Uriah.

JIP: You people really have become very different, you know.

URIAH: That is quite possible, that's army life for you.

JIP: But I am Jip, your comrade.

The three laugh. When Galy Gay also begins to laugh the others stop.

GALY GAY: One more ration. I'm ravenous now we're going into battle, and I like this fortress better and better.

Polly gives him a third dish.

JIP: Who is that gobbling up your rations?

URIAH: Mind your own business.

JESSE: You know, you couldn't possibly be old Jip. Old Jip would never have betrayed and abandoned us. Old Jip would never have let himself be held up. So you cannot be old Jip.

JIP: I certainly am.

URIAH: Prove it! Prove it!

JIP: Is there really not one of you who will admit he knows me? Then listen to me and mark my words. You are extremely hard-hearted men and your end can already be foreseen. Give me back my paybook.

GALY GAY *goes up to Jip with his last dish of rice*: You must be making a mistake. *Turns back to the others.* He's not right in the head. *To Jip:* Have you been going without food a lot? Would you like a glass of water? *To the others:* We shouldn't upset him. *To Jip:* Don't you know who you belong to? Never mind. Just sit down quietly over here till we have decided the battle. And please don't get any closer to the roar of the guns, as it demands great moral strength. *To the three:* He has no idea what's what. *To Jip:* Of course you need a pay-book. Nobody's going to let you run around without a pay-book, are they? Ah yes, Polly, look in the ammunition box where we keep the little megaphone and fish out Galy Gay's old papers, you remember, that fellow you used to tease me about. *Polly runs over to the box.* Anybody who has lived in the lowlands where the tiger asks the jaguar about his teeth knows how important it is to have something on you in black and white, because, you see, these days they are always trying to take your name away, and I know what a name is worth. O my children, when you called me Galy Gay that time, why didn't you just call me Nobody? Such larks are dangerous. They could have turned out very badly. But I always say let bygones be bygones. *He hands Jip the papers.* Here is that paybook, take it. Is there anything else you want?

JIP: You're the best of this lot. At least you've got a heart. But the rest of you will have my curse.

GALY GAY: To save you people having to listen to too much of that I'm going to make a bit of a noise with this gun for you . . . Show us how it works, Widow Begbick.

The two of them aim the gun at the fortress and start loading.

JIP: The icy wind of Tibet shall shrivel your bones to the marrow, you devils, never again shall you hear the harbour bell in Kilkoa, but shall march to the end of the world and back, over and over again. The Devil himself, your master, will have no use for you once you are old, and you will have to go on marching night and day through the Gobi desert and the waving green rye fields of Wales, and that shall be your recompense for betraying a comrade in need. *Exit.*

The three are silent.

GALY GAY: All set. And now I shall do it with five shots.

The first shot is fired.

BEGBICK *smoking a cigar*: You are one of those great soldiers who made the army so dreaded in bygone days. Five such men were a threat to any woman's life.

The second shot is fired.

I have proof that during the battle of the River Chadze it was by no means the worst elements in the company that dreamed of my kisses. One night with Leokadja Begbick was something for which men would sacrifice their whisky and save their shillings from two weeks' pay. They had names like Genghis Khan, famous from Calcutta to Couch Behar.

The third shot is fired.

One embrace from their beloved Irishwoman set their blood
to rights. You can read in *The Times* how staunchly they
fought in the battles of Bourabay, Kamatkura and Daguth.
The fourth shot is fired.

GALY GAY: Something that's no longer a mountain is tum-
bling down.

Smoke begins to pour from the fortress of Sir El-Djowr.

POLLY: Look!

Enter Fairchild.

GALY GAY: This is tremendous. Leave me alone now I've
tasted blood.

FAIRCHILD: What do you think you are doing? Take a look
over there. Right, I am now going to bury you up to the
neck in that anthill to stop you shooting the whole Hindu
Kush to pieces. My hand is steady as a rock. *He aims his
service pistol at Galy Gay.* It's not shaking at all. There, it is
plain as a pikestaff. You are now looking at the world for
the last time.

GALY GAY *loading enthusiastically*: One more shot! Just one
more. Just number five.

The fifth shot is fired. A cry of joy is heard from the valley below:
'The fortress of Sir El-Djowr that was blocking the pass
into Tibet has fallen. The army is advancing into Tibet.'

FAIRCHILD: Right. Once more I hear the familiar step of
the Army on the march, and now I propose to take a few
steps of my own. *Steps up to Galy Gay.* Who are you?

VOICE OF A SOLDIER *from below*: Who is the man who over-
threw the fortress of Sir El-Djowr?

GALY GAY: One moment. Polly, pass me that little megaphone out of the ammunition box, so I can tell them who it
is. *Polly fetches the megaphone and hands it to Galy Gay.*

GALY GAY *through the megaphone*: It was me, one of you,
Jeraiah Jip!

JESSE: Three cheers for Jeraiah Jip, the human fighting-
machine!

POLLY: Look!

The fortress has begun to burn. A thousand horrified voices cry out in the distance.

DISTANT VOICE: Flames are now engulfing the mountain fortress of Sir El-Djowr, in which seven thousand refugees from Sikkim province had found shelter, peasants, artisans and shopkeepers, most of them friendly, hard-working people.

GALY GAY: Oh. But what is that to me? The one cry and the other cry.

And already I feel within me
The desire to sink my teeth
In the enemy's throat
Ancient urge to kill
Every family's breadwinner
To carry out the conquerors'
Mission.

Hand me your paybooks.
They do so.

POLLY: Polly Baker.

JESSE: Jesse Mahoney.

URIAH: Uriah Shelley.

GALY GAY: Jeraiah Jip. At ease! We are now crossing the frontier of frozen Tibet.
Exeunt all four.

The Elephant Calf
An interlude for the foyer

Translator: JOHN WILLETT

Theatre

A few rubber trees above a trestle stage. Chairs in front of it.

POLLY *before the curtain*: In order that the act of the drama may have its full effect on you, you are invited to smoke like chimneys. Our artistes are the best in the world, our drinks over proof, our seats comfortable, bets on the story's outcome can be placed at the bars, acts will end and the curtain fall according to how the betting goes. Kindly do not take shots at the pianist, he is doing his best. Anyone who doesn't get the plot first go off needn't bother, it's incomprehensible. If you insist on seeing something full of meaning you should go to the gents. Ticket money will be refunded under no circumstances. Here is our comrade Jip, whose privilege it is to play the Elephant Calf, Jackie Pall. If that should strike you as impossibly difficult then all I can say is that stage artistes have got to be able to do absolutely anything.

SOLDIER *in audience*: Hear hear.

POLLY: Presenting Jesse Mahoney as the Elephant Calf's mother, with Uriah Shelley, the famous international turf expert, as the Moon. It will furthermore be your good fortune to see my humble self in the important role of the Banana Tree.

SOLDIERS: Get started, can't you? Fancy charging ten cents for rubbish like that.

POLLY: Permit me to inform you that we are absolutely impervious to crude interjections of that sort. The play is mostly about a crime committed by the Elephant Calf. I'm just telling you so that we don't have to keep interrupting.

URIAH *behind the curtain*: Alleged to have been committed.

POLLY: Quite right. That's because the only part I've read is my own. The Elephant Calf is innocent, you see.

SOLDIERS *slow clapping*: Get on with the show, get on with the show.

POLLY: All right, all right. *Steps behind the curtain.* You know I'm not sure we didn't charge too much for admission. What do you blokes think?

URIAH: Much too late to worry about that now. We just have to jump in at the deep end.

POLLY: It's such a feeble play, that's the difficulty. I'm sure you can't really remember, Jesse, how things went in the real theatre, and I rather think, Jesse, that what you've forgotten is the most important part of it. Here, half a mo', I've been taken short. *The curtain rises.* I am the Banana Tree.

SOLDIER: High time too.

POLLY: The arbiter of the jungle. I have been standing here on a parched savannah in South Punjab, yea ever since elephants were first invented. Now and then, but mainly in the evening, the Moon cometh to me to lay a complaint against an Elephant Calf, let's say.

URIAH: You're going too fast. You're half way there. It's ten cents, you know. *Enters.*

POLLY: Greetings, Moon, whence comest thou at this late hour?

URIAH: I have heard a good one about an Elephant Calf —

POLLY: Art laying a complaint against it?

URIAH: Aye, of course.

POLLY: So the Elephant Calf hath perpetrated a crime?

URIAH: It is precisely as thou supposest, indeed this is an instance of thy perspicacity from which naught can be hid.

POLLY: O, you've seen nothing yet. Hath not the Elephant Calf murdered his mother?

URIAH: Indeed he hath.

POLLY: Well, that's terrible.

URIAH: Appalling it is.

POLLY: If only I could find my specs.

URIAH: I just happen to have a pair on me, if they should fit you.

POLLY: They would fit all right if only they had lenses in them. Look, no lenses.

URIAH: Better than nothing, anyway.

POLLY: It's not a laughing matter.

URIAH: Aye, it is passing strange. Therefore I lay a complaint against the Moon, or rather the Elephant Calf.

Enter the Elephant Calf, slowly.

POLLY: Ah, here is that agreeable Elephant Calf. Whence comest thou, eh?

GALY GAY: I am the Elephant Calf. Seven Rajahs stood around my cradle. What are you laughing at, Moon?

URIAH: Keep talking, Elephant Calf.

GALY GAY: My name is Jackie Pall. I am taking a walk.

POLLY: They tell me thou didst beat thy mother to death.

GALY GAY: No, I just broke her milk jug to pieces.

URIAH: On her head, on her head.

GALY GAY: No, Moon, on a stone, on a stone.

POLLY: And I tell thee thou didst do it, as sure as I am a Banana Tree.

URIAH: And as sure as I am the Moon I shall prove it, and my first proof is this woman here.

Enter Jesse as the Elephant Calf's mother.

POLLY: Who's that?

URIAH: It's his mother.

POLLY: Isn't that rather peculiar?

URIAH: Not in the least.

POLLY: All the same it does strike me as peculiar her being there.

URIAH: Not me.

POLLY: Then she may as well stay, but of course you will have to prove it.

URIAH: Thou art the judge.

POLLY: All right, Elephant Calf, prove that thou didst not murder thy Mother.

SOLDIER *in the audience*: Hey, with her standing there . . .

URIAH *to the audience*: That's just the point.

SOLDIER: Even the start's a load of tripe. With his mother standing there. How on earth can the rest of the play be worth bothering about?

JESSE: I am the Elephant Calf's Mother, and I bet my little Jackie can prove quite conclusively that he's no murderer. Eh, Jackie?

URIAH: And I bet that he cannot and will not.

POLLY *bellows*: Curtain!

The audience goes silently to the bar and loudly and aggressively orders cocktails.

POLLY *behind the curtain*: That went very nicely, not a single boo.

GALY GAY: I'd like to know why nobody applauded?

JESSE: Perhaps they found it too gripping.

POLLY: But it's so interesting.

URIAH: If only we had a few chorus girls to flash their bums at them they'd tear up the seats. Get out in front, we must have a go at the betting lark.

POLLY *before the curtain*: Gentlemen . . .

SOLDIERS: Here, none of that. Let's have a proper interval. Give us time for a drink. A fellow needs it in this place.

POLLY: We just wanted to see if we could get you to lay a bet or two, on one of the two parties, that is, Mother versus Moon.

SOLDIERS: Bloody cheek. So that's their way of squeezing extra cash out of us. Just you wait till they get going. You ain't seen nothing yet.

POLLY: All right. Bets on the Mother, this side. *Nobody moves.* For the Moon, over here. *Nobody moves.*

URIAH *behind the curtain*: Have they placed their bets?

POLLY: Not so as you'd notice. They say that the best part's still to come, which I find most disturbing.

JESSE: They're drinking so appallingly, it's as if they couldn't sit through the rest otherwise.

URIAH: Sock them with a bit of music, that'll cheer them up.

POLLY *steps through the curtain*: Now for a few discs. *Withdraws. Curtain up.* Step forth, Moon, Mother and Elephant Calf, and ye shall learn the complete explanation of this mysterious crime, and you lot out there too. How dost thou hope to conceal the fact that thou, Jackie Pall, didst stab thine honourable Mother to death?

GALY GAY: How could I have done, seeing as how I am but a defenceless maiden?

POLLY: Art thou? Then let me put it to thee, Jackie Pall, that thou art by no means a maiden, as thou claimest. Now hark ye to my first major proof I recall a strange incident in my childhood in Whitechapel —

SOLDIER: South Punjab. *Roars of laughter.*

POLLY: — in South Punjab, when a fellow dressed up as a girl so as not to have to go off to the war. Up came the sergeant and tossed a round in his lap, and because he didn't move his legs apart, like a girl would to catch it in her skirt, the sergeant could tell he was a man, and the same thing here. *They do it.* There you are, now you all know the Elephant Calf's a man. Curtain! *Curtain. Feeble applause.*

POLLY: It's a smash hit, hear that? Curtain up! Take a bow! *Curtain. Applause stops.*

URIAH: They're positively nasty. It's all no use. The whole thing's hopeless.

JESSE: We must simply pack it in and refund their money. It's a matter of to be lynched or not to be lynched, that is the question; the situation is absolutely critical. Have a look out front.

URIAH: What, refund their money? Not on your life. There isn't a theatre in the world could stand that.

SOLDIERS: Tomorrow we'll be moving off to Tibet, eh, Georgie, may be the last time you ever sit under the rubber trees swigging four-cent cocktails. It's not particularly good weather for a war, or else it would be quite nice here, apart from this show.

SOLDIER: How about entertaining giving us a bit of a song, like 'Johnny Bowlegs, pack your kit and trek' say?

SOLDIERS: Bravo. *Sing 'Janny mit dem Hoppelbein'.*

URIAH: They've started their own singing now. We must get going again.

POLLY: I wish I were out there with them, 'Johnnys'' one of my favourite songs. Why couldn't we give them something like that? *Curtain up.* Now that . . . *He is competing with the singing.* Now that the Elephant Calf . . .

SOLDIER: Still going on about that Elephant Calf!

POLLY: As I was saying, now that the . . .

SOLDIER: Acting unpaid lance-calf.

POLLY: . . . That the animal in question has been exposed as a swindler by my first major proof, we move on to the second, even majorer proof.

SOLDIER: Can't we skip that one, Polly?

URIAH: Don't let them rattle you, Polly.

POLLY: I suggest that thou art a murderer, Elephant Calf. Therefore prove thine inability to murder, let's say, the Moon.

SOLDIER: That's not right. It's for the Banana Tree to do the proving.

POLLY: But that's just it. Now watch out. We've reached a particularly crucial point of the drama. As I was saying, thou must prove thine inability to murder, let's say, the Moon. Climb up this creeper of mine and take a knife with thee. *Galy Gay does so. The Moon holds the top of the rope ladder.*

SOLDIERS *quieten a few who want to continue singing*: Quiet! It's a tricky climb, you know, what with not being able to see out of that elephant's head.

JESSE: So long as he doesn't choose this moment to piss. Give it all you've got, Uriah. *Uriah gives a cry.*

URIAH: Oh, oh, oh!

POLLY: What's the matter, Moon, wherefore thy cries?

URIAH: Because it hurteth so. Emphatically this is a murderer climbing towards me.

GALY GAY: Hang the ladder on a branch, Uriah, I'm awfully weary.

URIAH: Oh, he is tearing my hand off. My hand! My hand! He is tearing off my hand.

POLLY: There you are, there you are.

Galy Gay has Uriah's artificial hand in his hands and shows it to the audience.

JESSE: That's bad, Jackie. I would not have thought it of thee. Thou art no child of mine.

URIAH *holds up stump of his hand*: I attest him to be a murderer.

POLLY: Behold the bleeding stump with which he attesteth; nor hast thou proved that it is impossible for thee to commit a murder, Elephant Calf, for now thou hast furthermore so handled the Moon that it must needs bleed to death before first light. Curtain! *Curtain. He immediately comes forward.* If anyone's interested in betting it can be done at the bar.

SOLDIERS *go to place bets*: A cent on the Moon, half a cent on the Elephant Calf.

URIAH: Look, they're starting to nibble. Now, Jesse, it's all yours with the sorrowing Mother's speech. *Curtain up.*

JESSE:

Do you all know what a mother is?
Ah, her heart is tender as no other is.
Tender your mother's heart as you lay in her
Tender the mother's hand that fed you dinner
Tender the mother's eye that watched you play
Tender the mother's foot that led the way
Laughter.
And when a mother's heart sinks beneath the sod
Laughter.
A noble soul goes shooting up to God.

Laughter.

Hear a mother, hear a mother weeping:

Laughter.

Mine is the bosom where this calf lay sleeping.

Stormy, prolonged laughter.

SOLDIERS: Encore! That alone's worth ten cents. Bravo! Hurrah! Three cheers for the Mother. Hip, hip, hooray!

Curtain falls.

URIAH: Carry on! It's a hit! Get on stage!

Curtain up.

POLLY: I have demonstrated that thou art a man capable of committing a murder. Now I put it to thee, Elephant Calf: art of the opinion that this is thy mother?

SOLDIERS: It's a damned unfair business, what they're performing up there, it absolutely goes against nature, it does. But very deep, very philosophical. They'll have some sort of happy ending up their sleeve, you bet. Quiet!

POLLY: Far be it from me to suggest, of course, that any child in the world would touch a hair of the head of the mother that bore him in any country under traditional British rule. *Hear, hear.* Rule Britannia! *All sing 'Rule Britannia'.* I thank you gentlemen. So long as this moving ditty resounds from rough masculine throats all will be well with England and her traditions. But on with the show! In as much as thou, O Elephant Calf, didst truly murder this universally beloved woman and great artiste – *Hear, hear –* it cannot possibly be the case that thou, Jackie Pall, art son or daughter of this celebrated lady – *Hear, hear –* moreover whatever a Banana Tree suggests he also proves. *Applause.* So take a piece of billiard chalk, thou Moon of Cooch Behar, and draw a firm circle in the centre of the stage. Thereupon take an ordinary rope in thy hand and wait until this profoundly stricken Mother steps into the middle of thy doubtless most incompetently drawn circle. Place the rope delicately round her white neck.

SOLDIERS: Round her lovely white mother's neck, round her lovely white mother's neck.

POLLY: Exactly. But thou, the alleged Jackie Pall, take the other end of this judicial rope and place thyself outside the circle over against the Moon. There; and now I ask thee, woman, didst thou give birth to a murderer? Art silent? Well, then. I just wanted to show you, gentlemen, that the mother herself, whom you see represented here, turns her back on her fallen child. But soon I shall show you even more, for soon the terrible sun of justice will be focussing its rays into the most hidden depths of this affair.

SOLDIERS: Don't overdo it, Polly. Sh!

POLLY: For the last time, Jackie Pall, dost persist in suggesting that thou art this wretched woman's son?

GALY GAY: Yes.

POLLY: Well, well. So thou art her son? A moment ago thou didst claim to be her daughter, but thou art not all that exact in thy statements. We shall now proceed, gentlemen, to our last and most important patent super-proof, which will not only surpass anything you have seen so far, but is guaranteed to give you total satisfaction. If thou, Jackie Pall, art this mother's child, then thou willst have been given the strength to pull thine alleged mother out of the circle to thy side. That's clear enough.

SOLDIERS: Crystal clear. Clear as a shithouse window. Hey, wait. He's got it all wrong. Just you stick to the truth, Jackie.

POLLY: When I count three, pull. *All count.* Go! *Galy Gay pulls Jesse out of the circle to his side.*

JESSE: Hey! Stop! Goddam! What d'you think you're up to? My neck!

SOLDIERS: What about it? Pull, Jackie! Stop! He's as blue as a fish out of water.

JESSE: Help!

GALY GAY: My side! my side!

POLLY: How about that, eh? Did you ever see such crude

behaviour? Now shall unnatural deception reap its reward. For thou hast clearly made a terrible mistake. By thy crude tugging hast thou proved, not what thou intendedst, but merely that under no circumstances cans't thou be son or daughter of this wretchedly tormented Mother. Thou hast made plain the truth, Jackie Pall.

SOLDIERS: Oho! Bravo! Stinking! Nice family, I don't think. Pack it in, Jackie, you've had it. Always tell the truth, Jackie.

POLLY: All right, gentlemen, I think that should do. That ought to look after our patent super-proof, I'd think. Now listen carefully, gentlemen, and I'd like those gentlemen to listen who saw fit to make a disturbance at the start of our show, and those who backed this miserable proof-riddled Elephant Calf with their good pence: this Elephant Calf is a murderer. The Elephant Calf, which is not the daughter of this honourable mother, as it suggested, but the son, as I have proved, and not the son either, as you saw, but simply no child whatsoever of this matron, whom it simply murdered, even though here she stands in full view of you all, acting as if nothing had happened, which is perfectly natural, even though previously unheard-of, as I can prove, and in fact I can now prove everything and am suggesting a great deal more and won't let myself be put off but insist on getting my certificate and even prove that, for I put it to you: what is anything without proof? *Steadily increasing applause*. Without proof men aren't men but orangutans, as proved by Darwin, and what about Progress, and just bat an eyelid, thou wretched little nonentity of a lie-sodden Elephant Calf, phoney to the very marrow, then I'll absolutely prove – in fact this is really the point of the whole thing, gentlemen – that this here Elephant Calf is no Elephant Calf whatsoever, but none other than Jeraiah Jip from Tipperary.

SOLDIERS: Hooray.

GALY GAY: It won't wash.

POLLY: And why not? Why won't it wash?

GALY GAY: Because it's not in the book. Take that back.

POLLY: Anyway, you're a murderer.

GALY GAY: That's a lie.

POLLY: But I can prove it. Prove it, prove it, prove it.

Galy Gay hurls himself with a groan at the Banana Tree whose base gives way under the force of his attack.

POLLY *falling*: See that? See that?

URIAH: All right, now you are a murderer.

POLLY *groaning*: And I proved it.

Curtain.

URIAH: Straight into the song, now.

The four players quickly take up positions before the curtain and sing.

> What a bit of all right in Uganda
> Seven cents a seat on the verandah
> And the poker games we played with that old tiger –
> No, I've never played as well as that.
> When we bet the hide off old Pa Krueger
> He bet nothing but his battered hat.
> > How peacefully the moon shone in Uganda!
> > Through the cool night we sat about
> > Until sunrise
> > And then pulled out.
> > A man needs money to be able
> > To sit at the poker table
> > With a tiger in disguise.
> > (Seven cents a seat on the verandah.)

SOLDIERS: Is it all over? It's a bloody travesty of justice. Call that a proper ending? You can't leave off like that. Keep the curtain up. Play on.

POLLY: What do you mean? We've come to the end of the script. Be reasonable, the play's over.

SOLDIERS: I never heard such a piece of cheek in all my life.

It's an absolute utter outrage, it offends every decent human instinct. *A compact group climbs on the stage and says seriously*: We want our money back. Either the Elephant Calf comes to a proper conclusion or else every single cent piece of ours must be on your table in two seconds, you Moon of Cooch Behar.

POLLY: It is our earnest submission that what we performed was the absolute truth.

SOLDIERS: All right, just you wait. We'll give you absolute truth.

POLLY: The fact is that you've no notion of art and no idea how artists should be treated.

SOLDIERS: Don't waste your breath.

GALY GAY: I wouldn't like you blokes to imagine I wouldn't stick up for what you've just seen, get me?

POLLY: Bravo, boss.

GALY GAY: Don't let's beat about the bush. Whichever of you is keenest to get his money back, let me just say I'd like to invite that particular phenomenon to step outside straight away for eight rounds with the four-ounce gloves.

SOLDIERS: Go on Towneley, see if you can wipe the floor with that Elephant Calf's little trunk.

GALY GAY: And now I fancy we'll see if what we performed was the absolute truth, or if it was good or bad theatre, my friends.

All off to the fight.

Notes and Variants

Texts by Brecht

THE MAN EQUALS MAN SONG

1

Hey, Tom, have you joined up too, joined up too?
'Cos I've joined up just like you, just like you.
And when I see you marching there
I know I'm back on the old barracks square
Have you ever seen me in your life?
'Cos I've never seen you in my life.
 It ain't the plan
 For man equals man
 Since time began.
 Tommy boy, let me tell you, it really ain't the plan
 For man is man!
 There's no other plan.
 The red sun of Kilkoa shines
 Upon our regimental lines
 Where seven thousand men can die
 And not a soul will bat an eye
 'Cos all the lot are better gone
 So who cares where Kilkoa's red sun shone?

2

Hey, Tom, was there rice in your Irish stew?
'Cos I had rice in my Irish stew
And when I found they'd left out the meat
The army didn't seem such a treat.
Hey, Tom, has it made you throw up yet?
'Cos I've not stopped throwing up as yet.
 It ain't the plan
 For man equals man

Since time began.
Tommy boy, let me tell you, it really ain't the plan
For man is man!
There's no other plan.
The red sun of Kilkoa shines
Upon our regimental lines
Where seven thousand men can die
And not a soul will bat an eye
'Cos all the lot are better gone
So who cares where Kilkoa's red sun shone?

3

Hey, Tom, did you see Jenny Smith last night?
'Cos me I saw Jenny Smith last night.
And when I look at that old bag
The army don't seem half such a drag.
Hey, Tom, have you also slept with her?
'Cos you know I've also slept with her.
　　It ain't the plan
　　For man equals man
　　Since time began.
　　Tommy boy, let me tell you, it really ain't the plan
　　For man is man!
　　There's no other plan.
　　The red sun of Kilkoa shines
　　Upon our regimental lines
　　Where seven thousand men can die
　　And not a soul will bat an eye
　　'Cos all the lot are better gone
　　So who cares where Kilkoa's red sun shone?

4

Hey, Tom, have you got your kit packed up?
'Cos I have got my kit packed up.
And when I see you with your kit
I feel the army's fighting fit.
But did you have bugger all to pack yours with?
'Cos I find I've bugger all to pack mine with.
　　It ain't the plan
　　For man equals man

Since time began.
Tommy boy, let me tell you, it really ain't the plan
For man is man!
There's no other plan.
The red sun of Kilkoa shines
Upon our regimental lines
Where seven thousand men can die
And not a soul will bat an eye
'Cos all the lot are better gone
So who cares where Kilkoa's red sun shone?

5

Hey, Tom, are you quite ready to move off?
'Cos me I'm quite ready to move off.
And when I see you march I guess
I'll march wherever the army says.
Have you got a clue where we're marching to?
'Cos I've not got a clue where we're marching to.
   It ain't the plan
   For man equals man
   Since time began.
   Tommy boy, let me tell you, it really ain't the plan
   For man is man!
   There's no other plan.
   The red sun of Kilkoa shines
   Upon our regimental lines
   Where seven thousand men can die
   And not a soul will bat an eye
   'Cos all the lot are better gone
   So who cares where Kilkoa's red shone?

['Der Mann-ist-Mann-Song,' from the 1927 edition of the play,
republished in GW *Gedichte*, pp. 138 ff. The former edition gives
Brecht's own tune, subsequently arranged by Paul Dessau.]

PRESS RELEASE

Disastrous prank by three privates of the Worchester Regiment
stationed at Kankerdan, East India/Prank? Or crime?/J. Galgei,
docker, takes himself for a soldier called Jerome Jip.

Saipong. All Hindustan is talking about the incredible case of J. Galgei,* a porter at the docks. Four private soldiers from Kankerdan, on detachment to Saipong, are alleged to have committed a hitherto baffling crime *in order to obtain whisky* (!!!), and to have been forced to abandon one of their number in the process. Realising that the absence of the fourth man might have betrayed the crime in question they camouflaged it by exploiting the person of the docker J. Galgei. Moved in the first place by mere sympathy, the latter was twice persuaded to stand in at roll calls for the missing man, one Jerome Jip. However when he cited family reasons and refused to oblige them for an additional two days till the unit moved off they cast him as the leading player in *a comedy worthy of the silver screen.* Along with a canteen proprietress of most dubious character they conspired to give him an alleged British army elephant free gratis and for nothing to sell as he might wish. Due to the unbridled consumption of whisky then prevalent Galgei failed to detect the true character of this dangerous gift: a highly life-like elephant constructed of nothing but some tarpaulins and his would-be benefactors the three privates. They thereupon arrested him for this 'theft' at the 'scene of the crime', and summarily shot him beneath the three sycamore trees of Saipong. They then revived this helplessly befuddled accomplice, who had fainted away well before his (obviously) faked execution, and told him he was to deliver a funeral oration on a certain Galgei who had just been shot. Now highly confused, he complied with all their demands and offered virtually no resistance. The following day too inspired peculiar misgivings in the unfortunate docker, who by now had become unsure of his own personality. Using an army paybook the soldiers brought their cruel game to its climax. Galgei's attitude to his wife, who had managed to track him down in his military guise, showed that at this point he was already uncertain of his own identity. As soon as the 'fun-loving' soldiers started making difficulties for him even with regard to his use of the name Jip, he so vehemently annexed that name that even the reappearance of the real Jip could not prise him away from it. Together with the simultaneous case of Sergeant P., who was so infuriated by the loss of self-control due to his unrestrained sexual urges as to castrate

* This was at a time when the three-day concentration of the Afghan Division provoked an enormous mêlée of soldiers and supply racketeers in Saipong, to say nothing of the less reputable camp followers associated with army units on the move.

himself with his own hand, this entire episode shows how thin the veneer of individuality has become in our time.

['Für Zeitungen,' from GW *Schriften zum Theater*, pp. 973 f. Prefaced to the 1925 typescript of the play.]

EPIC SEQUENCE OF EVENTS

The transformation of a living person in the Kilkoa military cantonment in the year nineteen hundred and twenty-five.

1

then they all joined together to make a false elephant and led the man galy gay unto it and bade him sell it but the sergeant came as he was holding it by a rope and they were afraid saying: what will he do? for they could not stay with him because of the sergeant and they observed him over a wall when he was alone to see if he would examine the elephant and notice that it was unreal however they saw that the man never looked at it and from thenceforward they knew that there was one who believed what was good for him and would sooner know nothing therefore he ignored the elephant not seeing that it was unreal for he wished to sell it and the woman that was with him took the sergeant away

2

so the man sold the elephant that was not his and was unreal to boot but thereupon one of them approached him laid his hand on his shoulder and spake to him: what art thou doing? and because he could not justify himself they brought suit against him but they condemned him to death then he denied that he was the criminal galy gay but they acted as if they believed him not and did shoot deceivingly at him from seven riflebarrels and he fainted and fell

3

however when he awakened they put a box before him telling him that the man galy gay who had been shot lay within it thereupon his reason became utterly confused and he began to think that he was not galy gay who had been shot and lay within the box nor did he wish to be wherefore he stood up and spake about galy gay as though he were a stranger that they might believe that he was not he for he feared to die and they buried the box which was empty and he delivered the funeral speech.

so they took him away with them that night

['Epischer Verlauf.' Fragment from BBA 348/68.]

Annex

a man was travelling in a train from kilkoa to tibet and they laid a woman beside him that he might sleep with her and ask no questions for they had told him that he was one of their men and when he woke he found the woman beside him but he knew her not then they said to him: who is the woman with whom thou hast slept? and he did not know for he had not slept with the woman but did not know it when they saw that he knew her not they mocked him saying perchance thou knowest not thyself then he said i know myself but he lied they however tested him in all ways and he was downcast and sat apart and knew not who he was but then he heard a voice behind the partition and a man began to lament and say what a disgrace has overtaken me where is my name that once was great beyond the oceans where is the yesterday that has vanished even my raiment is gone that i wore

[Untitled. BBA 150/151.]

TWO PARAGRAPHS

Execution

Galy Gay is led to the place of execution, but since he is being 'inconspicuously' led by Jesse and Polly – 'the disgrace for the regiment is too great; nothing of this must get out' – at first he is treated as a hero ('It's Jeraiah! Last-man-last-round Jip, the hero of Cochin Kula'). They all fête him; somebody asks him for a cigarette, hoping for reflected glory ('Happy to make your acquaintance. Wait till I tell them back home'). Then Uriah yells 'It's a mistake!' and they all learn that he is a deserter. Throw things at him, spit at him.

Recruitment

Camp whores are sent ahead to admire his uniform. Two quarrel over him. He could sleep with three girls if it weren't for the discovery of some small outward lapse, an undone button or a missing button or a missing shoulder-strap, which leads to the suspicion that he is a swindler.

['Die Erschiessung' and 'Die Werbung', from BBA 1080/75.]

INTRODUCTORY SPEECH (FOR THE RADIO)

Look: our plays embrace part of the new things that came into the world long before the world war. This means at the same time that they no longer embrace a large part of the old things to which we are accustomed. Why don't they now embrace these old things which *were* once recognised and proper? I think I can tell you exactly. They no longer embrace these old things because the people to whom these things were important are today on the decline. But whenever a broad stratum of humanity is declining its vital utterances get weaker and weaker, its imagination becomes crippled, its appetites dwindle, its entire history has nothing more of note to offer, not even to itself. What a declining stratum like this does can no longer lead to any conclusions about men's doings. In the case of the arts this means that such people can no longer create or absorb art of any sort.

This stratum of humanity had its great period. It created monuments that have remained, but even these remaining monuments can no longer arouse enthusiasm. The great buildings of the city of New York and the great discoveries of electricity are not of themselves enough to swell mankind's sense of triumph. What matters most is that a *new human type* should now be evolving, at this very moment, and that the entire interest of the world should be concentrated on his development. The guns that are to hand and the guns that are still being manufactured are turned for him or against him. The houses that exist and are being built are built to oppress him or to shelter him. All live works created or applied in our time set out to discourage him or to put courage in him. And any work that has nothing to do with him is not alive and has nothing to do with anything. This new human type will not be as the old type imagines. It is my belief that he will not let himself be changed by machines but will himself change the machine; and whatever he looks like he will above all look human.

I would now like to turn briefly to the comedy *Mann ist Mann* and explain why this introduction about the new human type was necessary. Of course not all these problems are going to arise and be solved in this particular play. They will be solved somewhere quite different. But it struck me that all sorts of things in *Mann ist Mann* will probably seem odd to you at first – especially what the central figure, the porter Galy Gay, does or does not do – and if so it's better that you shouldn't think you are listening to an old acquaintance talking or to yourself, as has hitherto nearly always been the rule in the theatre, but to a new sort of type, possibly an ancestor of just that new human type I spoke of. It may be interesting for you to look straight at him from this point of view, so as to find out his attitude to things as precisely as possible. You will see that among other things he is a great liar and an incorrigible optimist; he can fit in with anything, almost without difficulty. He seems to be used to putting up with a great deal. It is in fact very seldom that he can allow himself an opinion of his own. For instance when (as you will hear) he is offered an utterly spurious elephant which he can resell, he will take care not to voice any opinion of it once he hears a possible purchaser is there. I imagine also that you are used to treating a man as a weakling if he can't say no, but this Galy Gay is by no means a weakling; on the contrary he is the strongest of all. That is to say he becomes the strongest once he has ceased to be a private person; he only becomes strong in the mass. And if the play finishes up with him conquering an entire fortress this is only because in doing so he is apparently carrying out the determined wish of a great mass of people who want to get through the narrow pass that the fortress guards. No doubt you will go on to say that it's a pity that a man should be tricked like this and simply forced to surrender his precious ego, all he possesses (as it were); but it isn't. It's a jolly business. For this Galy Gay comes to no harm; he wins. And a man who adopts such an attitude is bound to win. But possibly you will come to quite a different conclusion. To which I am the last person to object.

['Vorrede zu *Mann ist Mann*' from *Die Szene*, Berlin, April 1927, reprinted in GW *Schiften zum Theater*, pp. 976 ff. This was an introductory talk to the broadcast of the play by Berlin Radio on March 27, 1927. It also appears in a shortened and adapted form as a statement by Brecht in the opening programme of Piscator's 1927–28 season. Part of another 'introductory speech' is included in GW *Schriften zum Theater* as well, but discusses the theatre in general rather than this particular play.]

DIALOGUE ABOUT BERT BRECHT'S PLAY *Man equals Man*

– Where have you been to put you in such a bad mood and so foul a temper?
– I've been to Bert Brecht's play Man equals Man and it's a bad play let me tell you and a waste of an evening.
– What makes you say that?
– Because it is a play that deals with ugly things such as are remote from me and the men in it are badly dressed and caked with the filth of their debased life such as is remote from me. And the plays I like are those in which moving or delightful things happen and clean well-dressed people perform.
– What's the good of being surrounded by moving or delightful things and clean well-dressed people if a red-hot lump of iron hits you and blots you out of life and the world?
– It is a play whose wit fails to make me laugh and its serious side to make me weep. And the plays I like are those in which the wit sparkles like fireworks or some sad occurrence moves my heart to compassion. For life is difficult and for a brief while I would fain be relieved of its burden.
– What's the good of enjoying wit like fireworks or having your heart moved at some sad occurrence if a red-hot lump of iron hits you and blots you out of life and the world?
– The plays I like are those that speak of the delights of Nature, of the freshness of springtime and the rushing of the wind through the trees in summer, of the pale sky in April and the last blossoms in autumn.
– What's the good of the freshness of springtime and the rushing of the wind through the trees in summer, of the pale sky in April and the last blossoms in autumn, if a red-hot lump of iron hits you and blots you out of life and the world?
– I take pleasure in beautiful women and I love the desire that comes from the sight of them as they laugh and move in plays and seduce men and are taken by them. For then I feel that I am a man and mighty in sex.

- What's the good of feeling desire at the sight of beautiful women as they laugh and seduce men and are taken by them and feeling that you are a man and mighty in sex if a red-hot lump of iron hits you and blots you out of life and the world?
- But I loathe whatever is degrading and disparaging and I feel myself raised to a higher plane by the nobility immanent in the plays of the great masters; I love whatever is lofty and improving, such as makes me sense the might of a God and the existence of a just Power.
- What's the good of being raised to a higher plane by nobility and feeling the might of a God and the existence of a just Power if a red-hot lump of iron hits you and blots you out of life and the world?
- Why do you have to go on repeating the same words in answer to all I've been saying about the beautiful and elevating things in the plays of the great masters?
- Because you too can get caught up like that man in Bert Brecht's play so as to blot out your name and your self and your home and your wife and your memory, your laughter and your passion, your desire for women and your elevation to God; because you too can be lined up like that man in a formation one hundred thousand strong, between man and man, dinner pail and dinner pail, just as millions of men have been lined up in the past and millions of men will be lined up in the future; because like that man you too can be hit by a red-hot lump of iron and blotted out of life and the world!!!
- *shouting*: Oh now I realise that it's a good play and its moral one to be taken to heart.

['Dialog zu Bert Brechts "Mann ist Mann"' from GW *Schriften zum Theater* p. 978. Date uncertain, but probably pre-1930.]

NOTES TO THE 1937 EDITION

1. About the direction

The comedy *Man equals Man* being a play of the parable type, unusual methods were adopted for its Berlin production. Stilts and wire clothes-hangers were used to turn the soldiers and their sergeant into exceptionally large and broad monsters. At the very end the porter Galy Gay was transformed into a monster of the same sort.

The four transformations were clearly distinguished from one another (transformation of Jeraiah Jip into a god; transformation of Sergeant Fairchild into a civilian; transformation of the canteen into an empty space; transformation of the porter Galy Gay into a soldier).

The components making up the set were like so many props. During Galy Gay's transformation two screens in the background – canvas stretched across large iron frames – showed pictures of Galy Gay before and after he had been transformed. Galy Gay was lying before the latter when he woke up again after being shot. The numbers of the separate stages in the transformation process were given by projections. The set was constructed in such a way that its appearance could be entirely changed by the removal of just a few of its components.

The 'Song of the Flow of Things' recited by the canteen proprietress during this transformation was accompanied by three kinds of activity. First, gathering the awnings: the canteen proprietress took a stick with an iron hook fixed to its end and gathered the two awnings together as she walked along the front of the stage reciting, her face turned towards the audience. Secondly, washing the awnings: she knelt in front of an opening in the stage and dipped the soiled pieces of linen into it, swirled them round as if in water and lifted out clean ones. Thirdly, folding the awnings: the canteen proprietress and the soldier Uriah Shelley held the awnings so they hung vertically right across the diagonal of the whole stage, and folded them together.

Sergeant Fairchild's transformation into a civilian (no. IVa [of scene 9]) was clearly marked off as an insertion by the half-curtain closing before and after it. The stage manager stepped forward with the script and read interpolated titles all through this process. At the start: 'Presenting an insertion: Pride and demolition of a great personality.' After the sentence 'Yes, because that is a civilian coming' [p. 55]: 'During the mobilisation Sergeant Fairchild visits the Widow Begbick on a personal matter.' After the sentence 'Stop you gob, civvy!': 'Nor did he learn from bitter experience. Clad as a civilian he staked his great military reputation to impress the widow.' After the sentence 'You really should, for my sake': 'In order to win the widow, he heedlessly demonstrated his skill as a shot.' After the sentence 'Eight women out of every nine would find this gory man divine': 'A famous episode was deprived of its shock effect.' After '. . . that for military reasons this canteen must be packed up': 'Though formally reminded of his duties, the sergeant insisted on having his will.' After '. . . or he'll demoralise the company': 'And so his inexplicable insistence on his private affairs caused him to forfeit his great name, the result of years of service.'

2. The Question of Criteria for Judging Acting

People interested in the ostensibly epic production of the play *Mann ist Mann* at the Staatsheater were of two opinions about the actor Lorre's performance in the leading part. Some thought his way of acting was perfectly right from the new point of view, exemplary even; others quite rejected it. I myself belong to the first group. Let me put the question in its proper perspective by saying that I saw all the rehearsals and that it was not at all due to shortcomings in the actor's equipment that his performance so disappointed some of the spectators; those on the night who felt him to be lacking in 'carrying-power' or 'the gift of making his meaning clear' could have satisfied themselves about his gifts in this direction at the early rehearsals. If these hitherto accepted hallmarks of great acting faded away at the performance (only to be replaced, in my view, by other hallmarks, of a new style of acting) this was the result aimed at by the rehearsals and is accordingly the only issue for judgement: the one point where opinions can differ.

Here is a specific question: How far can a complete change in the theatre's functions dislodge certain generally accepted criteria from their present domination of our judgement of the actor? We can simplify it by confining ourselves to two of the main objections to the actor Lorre mentioned above: his habit of not speaking his meaning clearly, and the suggestion that he acted nothing but episodes.

Presumably the objection to his way of speaking applied less in the first part of the play than in the second, with its long speeches. The speeches in question are his protest against the announcement of the verdict, his pleas before the wall when he is about to be shot, and the monologue on identity which he delivers over the coffin before its burial. In the first part it was not so obvious that his manner of speaking had been split up according to gests, but in these long summings-up the identical manner seemed monotonous and to hamper the sense. It hardly mattered in the first part that people couldn't at once recognise (feel the force of) its quality of bringing out the gest, but in the second the same failure of recognition completely destroyed the effect. For over and above the meaning of the individual sentences a quite specific basic gest was being brought out here which admittedly depended on knowing what the individual sentences meant but at the same time used this meaning only as a means to an end. The speeches' content was made up of contradictions, and the actor had not to make the spectator identify himself with individual sentences and so get caught up in contradictions, but to keep him out of them. Taken as a whole it had to be the most objective possible exposition of a contradictory internal process. Certain particularly significant sentences were therefore 'highlighted', i.e. loudly declaimed, and their selection amounted to an intellectual achievement (though of course the same could also be the result of an artistic process). This was the case with the sentences 'I insist you put a stop to it!' and 'It *was* raining yesterday evening!' By these means the sentences (sayings) were not brought home to the spectator but withdrawn from him; he was not led but left to make his own discoveries. The 'objections to the verdict' were split into separate lines by caesuras as in a poem, so as to bring out their character of adducing one argument after another; at the same time the fact that the individual arguments never followed logically on one another had to be appreciated and even applied. The impression intended was of a man simply reading a case for the defence prepared at some quite different period, without understanding what it meant as he did so. And this was indeed the impression left on any of the audience who knew how to make such observations. At first sight, admittedly, it was possible to overlook the truly magnificent way in which the actor Lorre delivered his inventory. This may seem peculiar. For generally and quite rightly the art of not being overlooked is treated as vital; and here are we, suggesting that something is magnificent which needs to be hunted for and found. All the same, the epic theatre has profound reasons for insisting on such a reversal of criteria. Part of the social transformation of the theatre is that the spectator should not be worked on in the usual way. The theatre is no longer the place where his interest is aroused but where he brings it to be satisfied. (Thus our ideas of tempo have to be revised for the epic theatre. Mental processes, e.g., demand quite a different tempo from emotional ones, and cannot necessarily stand the same speeding-up.)

We made a short film of the performance, concentrating on the principal nodal points of the action and cutting it so as to bring out the gests in a very abbreviated way, and this most interesting experiment shows surprisingly well how exactly Lorre manages in these long speeches to mime the basic meaning underlying every (silent) sentence. As for the other objection, it may be that the epic theatre, with its wholly different attitude to the individual, will simply do away with the notion of the actor who 'carries the play'; for the play is no longer 'carried' by him in the old sense. A certain capacity for coherent and unhurried development of a leading part, such as distinguished the old kind of actor, now no longer matters so much. Against that, the epic actor may possibly need an even greater range than the old stars did, for he has to be able to show his character's coherence despite, or rather by means of, interruptions and jumps. Since everything depends on the development, on the flow, the various phases must be able to be clearly seen, and therefore separated; and yet this must not be achieved mechanically. It is a matter of establishing quite new rules for the art of acting (playing against the flow, letting one's characteristics be defined by one's fellow-actors, etc.). The fact that at one point Lorre whitens his face (instead of allowing his acting to become more and more influenced by fear of death 'from within himself') may at first sight seem to stamp him as an episodic actor, but it is really something quite different. To begin with, he is helping the playwright to make a point, though there is more to it than that of course. The character's development has been very carefully divided into four phases, for which four masks are employed – the packer's face, up to the trial; the 'natural' face, up to his awakening after being shot; the 'blank page', up to his reassembly after the funeral speech; finally the soldier's face. To give some idea of our way of working: opinions differed as to which phase, second or third, called for the face to be whitened. After long consideration Lorre plumped for the third, as being characterised, to his mind, by 'the biggest decision and the biggest strain'. Between fear of death and fear of life he chose to treat the latter as the more profound.

The epic actor's efforts to make particular incidents between human beings seem striking (to use human beings as a setting), may also cause him to be misrepresented as a short-range episodist by anybody who fails to allow for his way of knotting all the separate incidents together and absorbing them in the broad flow of his performance. As against the dramatic actor, who has his character established from the first and simply exposes it to the inclemencies of the world and the tragedy, the epic actor lets his character grow before the spectator's eyes out of the way in which he behaves. 'This way of joining up', 'this way of selling an elephant', 'this way of conducting the case', do not altogether add up to a single unchangeable character but to one which changes all the time and becomes more and more clearly defined in course of 'this way of changing'. This hardly strikes the spectator who is used to something else. How many spectators can so far discard the need for tension as to see how, with this new sort of actor, the same gesture is used to summon him to the wall to change his clothes as is subsequently used to summon him there in order to be shot, and realise that the situation is similar but the behaviour different? An attitude is here required of the spectator which roughly corresponds to the reader's habit of turning back in order to check a point. Completely different economies are needed by the epic actor and the dramatic. (The actor Chaplin, incidentally, would in many ways come closer to the epic than to the dramatic theatre's requirements.)

It is possible that the epic theatre may need a larger investment than the ordinary theatre in order to become fully effective; this is a problem that needs attention. Perhaps the incidents portrayed by the epic actor need to be familiar ones, in which case historical incidents would be the most immediately suitable. Perhaps it may even be an advantage if an actor can be compared with other actors in the same part. If all this and a good deal more is needed to make the epic theatre effective, then it will have to be organised.

3. Making the play concrete

The parable *Man equals Man* can be made concrete without much difficulty. The transformation of the petty-bourgeois Galy Gay into a 'human fighting-machine' can take place in Germany instead of India. The army's concentration at Kilkoa can be made into the Nazi party rally at Nuremberg. The elephant Billy Humph can be replaced by a stolen motor-car now the property of the SA. The break-in can be located in a Jewish junk dealer's shop in lieu of Mr Wang's temple. The shopkeeper then engages Jip to be his Aryan partner. The ban on damaging Jewish shops could then be explained by the presence of English journalists.

[From Brecht *Gesammelte Werke*, London 1937, vol 1, pp. 220–224. Of the three sections, 1 refers to the 1931 production; 2 reprints Brecht's letter to the *Berliner Börsen-Courier* of 8 March of that year; while 3 dates from 1936. The SA or Storm Detachments were Hitler's brownshirts. The term 'Aryan' was used by the Nazis to denote non-Jewish.]

ON LOOKING THROUGH MY FIRST PLAYS (v)

I turned to the comedy *Man equals Man* with particular apprehension. Here again I had a socially negative hero who was by no means unsympathetically treated. The play's theme is the false, bad collectivity (the 'gang') and its powers of attraction, the same collectivity that Hitler and his backers were even then in the process of recruiting by an exploitation of the petty-bourgeoisie's vague longing for the historically timely, genuinely social collectivity of the workers. Before me were two versions, the one performed at the Berlin Volksbühne in 1928 and the other at the Berlin Staatstheater in 1931. I decided to restore the earlier version, where Galy Gay captures the mountain fortress of Sir El-Djowr. In 1931 I had allowed the play to end with the great dismantling operation, having been unable to see any way of giving a negative character to the hero's growth within the collectivity. I decided instead to leave that growth undescribed.

But this growth into crime can certainly be shown, if only the performance is sufficiently alienating. I tried to further this by one or two insertions in the last scene.

[From 'Bei Durchsicht meiner ersten Stücke.' GW *Schriften zum Theater*, p. 951. Written in March 1954 and originally forming part of the introduction of *Stücke I* and *II.*]

Editorial Notes

1. EVOLUTION OF THE PLAY

The name Galy Gay and the basic idea of one man being forced to
assume the personality of another both derive from the *Galgei* project which Brecht appears to have conceived as early as 1918 and
begun developing in spring or early summer of 1920. 'In the year
of Our Lord . . .', says a diary note of 6 July 1920,

> citizen Joseph Galgei fell into the hands of bad men who mal-
> treated him, took away his name and left him lying skinless.
> Everyone should look to his own skin.

It was to be 'just the story of a man whom they break (they have
to) and the sole problem is how long can he stand it . . . They lop
off his feet, chuck away his arms, bore a hole in his head till the
whole starry heaven is shining into it: is he still Galgei? It's a sex
murder story.'

This play was to have been set in Augsburg, and its theme was
how 'Galgei replaces Pick the butter merchant for a single evening'. An early scheme specifies eight scenes, thus:

1. In the countryside. Pick's death.
2. The Plärrer [i.e. the Augsburg fair]. Galgei's abduction.
3. The Shindy Club. Dagrobu [?meaning]. Pick's funeral. Galgei.
4. Ma Col's bedroom. Galgei half saved. The big row.
5. River. Murder of Galgei. His rescue.
6. Next morning at the club.
7. Galgei's house. Galgei's burial.
8. In the countryside. Pick's resurrection.

A fragmentary text of the first three scenes shows Pick going off
in dudgeon; a splash is then heard. Scene 2 is described as '*Big*

swing-boats. Evening. Violet sky' and opens with the news of Pick's death:

> MATTHI: Who is going to pay Pick's taxes and emit Pick's farts?

Galgei, a fat man, is on the swings; by profession he is a carpenter. A bystander describes him:

> He is a most respectable man. Lives quietly and modestly with his wife. He's behaving very childishly today. It's the music. He's such a reliable worker.

Scene 3 at the Shindy Club's subterranean bar is subdivided into episodes. Ma Col (a proto-Begbick) is behind the bar polishing glasses. Enter Galgei with Ligarch, the club president, who was on the swings with him. Shaking hands, he says 'I must remain what I am. But I'm in top form tonight . . .', and there it breaks off. However, a slightly more detailed scheme than the first one takes it on:

> Galgei gatecrashes the Shindy Club. 1. He wants to ingratiate himself. 2. He takes part in the business. 3. He hasn't got a woman. 4. He takes the butter business over.

– while the remaining scenes are developed in a slightly different order thus:

> 4. Bedroom, white calico. Love.
>   *The screws are tightened.* Galgei is caught.
>   i. He falls in love with Ma Col.
>   ii. He gets money. Hunger.
>   iii. He falls out with Matthi.
>   iv. He goes to the butter business.
> 5. Bar. Brown. Beasts of prey. Schnaps.
>   *He is transformed.* The big row in the club. Galgei feels that he is Pick.
>   i. He fights for Ma Col.
>   ii. He stands up for Salvarsan.
>   iii. He abandons Lukas.
> 6. River meadows, green weeds, fat bodies.
>   *He turns nasty.*
>   i. He murders Matti.
>   ii. He is overcome by doubt.

7. Bar.
   i. He wakes up.
   ii. He consoles Ma Col until he is at home.

A further sketch for scene 8 describes the setting as '*River. Dawn light. Distant sound of bells.*' and has Ligarch saying to Galgei 'Come. Today God is in Chicago. The sky is displaying the *cruel* constellations.'

Like Shlink in *In the Jungle*, a play which Brecht was only to start planning a year or more later, Galgei was supposed to lose his skin. He was fat and passive, so a note of May 1921 suggests, with

a red wrinkled skin, particularly on his neck, close-cropped hair, watery eyes and thick soles. He seethes inwardly and cannot express himself. But everything derives from the fact that people look towards him.

This 'lump of flesh' was to be like a jellyfish, an amorphous life-force flowing to fill whatever empty shape was offered it. It was like 'a donkey living who is prepared to live on like a pig. The question: Is he then living?

Answer: He is lived.

'What I'm not sure of,' reflected Brecht, 'is whether it is at all possible to convey the monstrous mixture of comedy and tragedy in Galgei, which lies in the fact of exposing a man who can be so manipulated and yet remain alive.'

From then on the project seems to have stagnated, only to be revived in the summer of 1924 when Brecht was about to leave Bavaria for Berlin. The Augsburg context was now discarded, to be replaced by an Anglo-Indian setting derived from Brecht's interest in Kipling and first foreshadowed in a story and poem about 'Larrys Mama', the 'mummy' in question being the British (or Indian) army. The first version of the new scheme specifies no less than fifteen scenes as follows:

1. galgei goes to buy a fish. 2. Soldiers lose fourth man. 3. buy galgei. 4. have to do without fourth man. 5. galgei plays jip. 6. jip's betrayal. 7. billiards. 8. elephant scene. 9. flight. 10.

execution. 11. departure. 12. train on the move. 13. jip. 14. mime, niggerdance, boxing match. 15. general clean-up.

– also mentioning 'Blody Five', a 'Saipong Song' and such key phrases as 'the gentleman who wishes not to be named', '1 = 0' [einer ist keiner] and 'there must be two souls in you', the old Faustian principle. Starting on his own, then later with Elisabeth Hauptmann's help. Brecht completed this to make the first full version of the play, an extremely long text which included the whole of *The Elephant Calf*, more or less as we now have it, as the penultimate scene. The characters at first included besides Galgei: John Cakewater (or Cake), Jesse Baker (or Bak), Uria Heep (presumably after Dickens) and Jerome Jip as the four soldiers, and Leokadja Snize as the canteen lady, with a daughter called Hiobya. In the course of the writing, however, these names gave way respectively to Galy Gay, Jesse Cakewater, Polly Baker, Uria Shelley, Jeraiah Jip, and Leokadja and Hiobya Begbick. The sergeant remained Blody Five throughout. Saipong, the original setting, became Kilkoa, and at some point in 1925 Brecht decided that the play's title would be *Galy Gay or Man = Man*.

Bound in with the script of this version is a good deal of miscellaneous material, which sets the tone thus:

the three knockabouts
the worst blokes in the indian army
the golden scum
knife between the teeth gents
you people stand in the corner when he comes in and smile horribly (this happens)

A discarded episode between Bak and Galgei goes:

bak: some people live like in a marriage ad to put it scientifically their excrement is odourless but there are those who look life straight in the eye i don't know if you've ever felt the carnal pepper in you i'm talking about unchastity
galgei: i know what you mean
bak: have you ever handled a woman with paprika i'll never forget how a woman once bit me on the tit because i didn't beat her quite long enough
galgei: she liked your beating her did she

bak: that's not so uncommon but don't put on an act with me i
  bet you're just as ready to give your flesh its head in that sort
  of situation don't tell me a man with a face like yours isn't
  sensitive to the impressions one can pick up in gents' urinals
  say
galgei: i must tell you that in the circumstances i find it difficult
  to put up with your remarks
bak: take a good look at your innermost self do you feel any
  impulse say to hit me in the face?
galgei: just a fleeting one
bak: look the other way i get too excited when you look at me
  excuse me

on another occasion someone describes a peculiarly bloody battle
scene their hair stands on end as they sing like drunks he quivers
like a rabbit

the scum is bawling

every spring blood has to flow

jabyourknifeintohimjackhiphiphurrah

It ends with two significant phrases: 'they bank on him entirely,
will go to the stake for him' and 'he is ready to become a murderer,
saint, merchant'. A third – 'He cannot say no' – comes in a slightly
later scheme. There is also an unrealised idea for 'Galgay [*sic*]
choruses':

> All those who do far too much
> Have no time for sleeping
> Have no longer a cold hand
> For their best crimes
> Whatever happens
> Under the sun and under the moon
> Is as good as if
> Sun and moon were thoroughly used to it
> You'll see three soldiers in Kilkoa
> Commit an offence
> And when night came with its dangers
> You saw them go to bed

But there are other criminals who
Bear Cain's mark on their brows
Before nightfall
Seated at the bicycle races
But these go to bed
So do not lose heart
For the moon goes on shining
While they are provisionally asleep
And next day they'll step with old
Feet into new water
For they are not always present
But leave the wind blowing through the bushes for one night
And the moon shining for one night
And next day look out on
Changed world

The first published version is dated 1926 and bears the final title *Mann ist Mann*. It represents a reduced and somewhat subdued revision of its 1924/5 predecessor, with the penultimate scene now separated as an appendix under the title *The Elephant Calf or The Provability of Any Conceivable Assertion*; the direction saying that it should be performed in the foyer only came later. This text, which doubtless bears a close relationship to that of the play's premières the same year, has been translated in full by Eric Bentley in the Grove Press *Seven Plays by Bertolt Brecht* (1961 – to be distinguished from later Grove Press editions where the play has been adapted). The original Ullstein (Propyläen) edition also gives melody and piano accompaniment for the 'Man equals Man Song' which seems to have developed out of the Saipong Song mentioned earlier. An amended version of this text was used for Erich Engel's 1928 production at the Volksbühne, after which Arkadia (another offshoot of the Ullstein publishing empire) issued a duplicated stage script. This in turn formed the basis of Brecht's own production with Peter Lorre at the Staatstheater in 1931. The major changes made up to this point included the cutting of Begbick's three daughters Hiobya, Bessie and Ann, who are described in the 1926 version as 'half-castes who form a jazz band', and an extensive reshuffling of lines between the three soldiers. Our scenes 4 and 5 were run into one and scenes 6 and 7 were cut, while in our long scene 9 the soldiers were to sing the Mandalay Song (as in *Happy End*) and the Cannon Song (as in the *Threepenny Opera*) finishing up with the

Man equals Man Song and a very short final scene. For Brecht's production however Begbick's Interlude speech was shifted to form a prologue, its place being taken by Jesse's speech 'I tell you, Widow Begbick' on p. 41, which was to be delivered 'before the portrait of Galy Gay as a porter'. Blody Five was changed to *Blutiger Fünfer* (Bloody Fiver) throughout; it will be seen how as a character he diminishes. Both the Man equals Man Song and the Song of Widow Begbick's Drinking Car were thrown out, but a new Song of the Flow of Things (stylistically very close to the 'Reader for Those who Live in Cities' poems) was brought in instead of the interpolated songs in scene 9. The play ended with the soldiers entraining as at the end of that scene. The programme described it as a 'parable'.

This in turn formed the basis for the second published version, that of the Malik collected edition in 1938. Its text is the same as ours up to the end of Galy Gay's long verse speech in scene 9 (v), after which a slight shuffling of the dialogue, followed by a final brief speech from Galy Gay, allowed the play to end with that scene. In 1954, however, 'on looking through his first plays' for Suhrkamp's new collected edition, Brecht decided to bring back scenes 10 and 11 from the 1926 version, modifying them slightly so as to include the final brief speech of 1938, which now occurs on p. 76. The result was the text which we now have. But of course Brecht never saw it staged in this form, and no doubt he would have modified it yet again. For all his plays there was scarcely one that he found so difficult to let alone. All in all, he once wrote, 'from what I learnt from the audiences that saw it, I rewrote *Man equals Man* ten times'. Looking at the material in the Brecht Archive one soon loses count. But it is easy to believe that he spoke the truth.

2. NOTES ON INDIVIDUAL SCENES

Scene numbers and titles are given as in our version of the play. Numbers in square brackets refer to those in whichever text is under discussion.

1. Kilkoa

The 1924/5 text describes the setting simply as *'road'*. Otherwise this scene has remained unchanged apart from the wife's final line:

Please don't wander around. I am going to bolt myself into the kitchen so you needn't be worried on account of all those idle soldiers.

This survived till 1931 and was then cut.

2. Street outside the Pagoda of the Yellow God

The 1924/5 text has a version of his scene which finishes after 'I'm hanging by the hair' (p. 7) and appears to have been added after the writing of the following scene. In it Uria refers to the army as 'Mummy':

> the army whom we call mummy and who sends her sons to such towns half way across india pays them two and a half bottles of whisky per head.
>
> JESSE: nothing's stronger than mummy.

The opening stage direction specifies '*four soldiers and a machine-gun marching to their camp on whisky*'. The 1926 published version has them also singing the Man equals Man Song, but in both texts the talk throughout is of whisky rather than beer. The 1926 version differs also from our text in (a) its omission of all Jesse's opening speech after 'Kilkoa!' (p. 4): instead he continues with the words now given to Polly ('Just as the powerful tanks' etc.); (b) the wording of the first attempt to break into the temple; and (c) its omission of the paybook episode (pp. 5–6).

[*2, amended to 3. in the huts, evening. cake, bak, heep, hiobja sneeze.*]

This is in the 1924/5 version only and was later absorbed in our scenes 3 and 4. There are two alternatives for this short scene, the second of which is marked 'Written by Hesse Burri to dictation' (i.e. presumably Brecht's). In the first Hiobja, who is also known as Hipsi, talks to the three soldiers as the 'wanted' notice is being put up, and calls Blody 5 'the devil of saipong'. His voice is then heard bawling out the men:

> call those trousers? what? i'll have you scrubbing the shithouse with a toothbrush till your hair turns white, you swine!

Rations are doled out and Jip's portion falls on the floor as there
is no one to take it. Blody asks 'where is your fourth man?' as at
the top of p. 9. The three then agree that they must find him
before nightfall, and the text breaks off. A page of notes follows
with phrases like 'the hell of kilkoa', 'begbick and bloodsucker',
'two cents a chair', 'one full whisky', 'our skins are at stake' and
'the fragile rocking-chair', then a fresh start with

canteen. evening. hiobja begbick, soldiers

The soldiers sing 'In Widow Begbick's Splendid Drinking Truck',
and one Jack Townley (see the end of the *Elephant Calf*) complains
about the prices and says:

> i jack townley who unlike you footsloggers and gun-tuggers
> know such a metropolis as cairo like the back of my hand can
> only tell you i must have been in some 1500 gin- rum- and
> alebars there with say between two and five ladies on each
> storey but so sinful an establishment as this is more than jack
> ever . . .

Enter then the three, who are asked by the others about their missing fourth man. They buy drinks all round and are charged two
cents per chair, one of which breaks. The 'Wanted' notice goes up
and the sergeant's voice is heard cursing the men and announcing
the Afghan campaign:

> i knew we'd be getting the scum of every regiment but now
> i come to look at you it's far worse than i thought it's my con-
> sidered opinion that you're the most plague-ridden bunch of
> throwouts that ever wore its boots out in the queen's service
> today i observed some individuals among the huts laughing
> in such a carefree way that it chilled me to the marrow i know
> who they are and let me tell you there will be one or two hairs
> in *their* christmas pudding

The rations are doled out; the sergeant asks about the missing
fourth man, and the scene breaks off, all much as before.

3. Country Road between Kilkoa and the Camp

In the 1924/5 text this is marked 'brecht first version' and described as 'deserted road. galgei carries leokadja begbick's cucumber

basket for her'. It starts with the entrance of Begbick and Galy
Gay, much as on our p. 9, and has two alternative endings of
which the second is close to our version. The 1926 added the beginning of the scene somewhat as we now have it, taken from the
abandoned canteen scene above. The rest of the scene was slightly
revised and extended, leaving only a few lines to be added in the
1938 version to arrive at the present text.

4. Canteen of the Widow Leokadia Begbick

The 1924/5 scene 4 is set '*in the cantonment. night. leokadja. hiobja.
roll-call off.*' The three soldiers are worried as now that if it rains
Jip's palanquin will be taken indoors, so they go off with Begbick's
scissors, leaving her and Galy Gay to discuss whether he was or
was not the man who carried her cucumber. They make no serious
approach as yet to Galy Gay.

The 1926 version starts as now, with material from the second
part of the abandoned scene above. The opening song is accompanied by Begbick's three half-caste daughters, after which the
dialogue (p. 14) is allocated rather differently from now, so that it
is the soldiers who inquire about the missing man and say that the
sergeant is 'not nice', while it is Hiobja ('thou flower on the dusty
path of the soldiery', as her mother calls her) who describes the
sergeant's habits:

> They call him Blody Five, the Tiger of Kilkoa. His hallmark
> is The Human Typhoon. His warcry on seeing a man ripe for
> the Johnny-are-you-dry wall is 'Pack your suitcase, Johnny.'
> He's got an unnatural sense of smell, he smells out crime. And
> each time he smells one he sings out 'Pack your suitcase,
> Johnny.'

– a reference, surely, to the line 'Johnny Bowlegs, pack your kit
and trek' in Kipling's 'Song of the Banjo', which in turn derived
from the South African song 'Pack your kit and trek, Ferrera'. The
phrase recurs throughout this version of the play.

The appeal to Galy Gay which follows (p. 15) is much as now
except that it is all given to Polly and Galy Gay's speech on entering is omitted. The other soldiers do not exit, but remain to comment; Galy Gay is not undressed; and the bargaining over the
uniform is somewhat shorter. Begbick's account of the effect of

rain on the sergeant is the same as now from 'Not a bit of it' (p. 18) to 'as a kitten', but goes on to end

> For when it rains Blody Five turns into Blody Gent and for three days the bloody gent only bothers about girls.

On Galy Gay's departure after the announcement of the roll-call there is no further bargaining (down to p. 19), nor are Polly's speech to Begbick and her seductive preparations included. Instead she tells Hiobja to put the tarpaulin over the waggon, after which Blody enters *'appallingly transformed'* and listens to the roll-call outside:

> BLODY: You're laughing. But let me tell you I'd like to see this all go up in flames, this Sodom with its bar and its rocking chair, and you who are a one-woman Gomorrah. Don't cast such devouring glances at me, you whitewashed Babylon.
>
> LEOKADJA: You know, Charlie, a woman likes to see a man being so passionate.

There is no verse speech by Begbick, and Blody goes on with his next speech as now, down to 'one means business' (p. 20), after which the voice off summons the MG section, so that there is no reference to Blody dressing in a bowler hat. The remainder is much as now, except that there is no verse speech by Galy Gay and no song by Begbick at the end, nor does Uriah provide beer and cigars. The song comes in the 1931 stage version, where it is sung through a megaphone. In 1926 Polly says 'Drink a few cocktails and put them down to us', which Galy Gay then proceeds to do. The scene ends with his denying having carried Begbick's basket, and Begbick saying 'It's begun to rain'.

5. Interior of the Pagoda of the Yellow God [misnumbered 6 in the 1926 edition which specifies that the sacristan is Chinese. Cut in the Arkadia scripts of 1929–30.]

The 1924/5 version is close to our text, except that after 'seem to slumber very well' (p. 24) Uriah goes on to say:

> i am sure you would be ashamed to tell a lie and here are 3 revolvers what's more made by everett & co each containing 6 bullets i am sure you would not wish to contain 6 bullets as you are not a revolver

– whereupon the sacristan aims a rifle at him. Wang shouts 'fire!'
and the sacristan runs away.

The rest of the scene, with the drawing of the four men, is virtually as now. In the Arkadia scripts this is the only part to be retained; it is taken into the canteen scene when Wang enters to
order drink.

6. The canteen [7 in the 1926 edition. Cut in the Arkadia scripts, but
restored in modified form for the 1931 production.

This scene remained unchanged since 1926 and would be almost
the same in the 1924/5 version too but for the omission of Jesse's
and Polly's concluding remarks. It concludes with Baker saying
after 'a mere thread' (p. 26):

> I shan't say anything more to him tonight.
> *Galgay yawns in his sleep and makes himself comfortable.*

7. Interior of the Pagoda of the Yellow God [8 in the 1926 edition. Cut
in the Arkadia scripts].

In the 1924/5 version this comes after the next canteen scene, but
it is almost word for word as now apart from the substitution of
beer for the original whisky. The 1926 text is even closer.

The 1931 text simply showed Jip outside the pagoda surrounded
by beer bottles and a large plate of meat, and had him deliver a
verse speech paraphrasing his concluding speech here:

> What am I, Jeraiah Jip from Tipperary, to do
> When I'm told our entire army
> Twelve railway trains and four elephant parks
> Moved over the Punjab Mountains during the past month?
> Here however I can eat meat and drink beer
> My ten bottles a day, and in return have only to
> Look after the temple that there are no further incidents
> And get my food and get my beer and get my
> Orderly existence. True
> I ought to go and help them
> In their life's worst quandary, since I after all
> Am their fourth man. But why
> Does meat taste so good and
> Is beer so essential? True, Jesse will say 'Jip's sure to come.'
> Once he's sober Jip will come.

But this beefsteak suits me, good meat.
Uriah may not wait quite so patiently since
Uriah is a bad man.
Jesse and Polly will say 'Jip's sure to come.' But
Must a man abandon meat like this?
Can he go away? If he's hungry?
No, no. He mustn't if he cannot.

8. The canteen.

The 1924/5 version, like the 1926 published text, has Galy Gay
half asleep while the three soldiers play billiards. The scene follows
on scene 6 and starts with Polly's comment 'He must be frozen
stiff' (p. 30), then they wake Galy Gay up and continue approximately with the dialogue from 'Dear Sir' (p. 31) to where Galy
Gay wants to leave (p. 32), Uriah's speech about the joys of army
life being marked by Brecht 'written by Hesse Burri in Augsburg'.
Next it appears that Galy Gay wants to rejoin his wife:

> CAKE: of course he needs a woman the fellow's like an elephant
> URIAH: he can get one with his next week's pay
> BAK: i'll go with him myself and select one so he doesn't go
> sick
> CAKE: meantime he can do it with begbick

Enter Blody 5, who brings in the wife (p. 35), after which the
dialogue is roughly as now up to the wife's exit (p. 37), after
which the soldiers congratulate themselves:

> URIAH: it's an honour for us to have a man like you in the unit.
> GALY GAY: the honour's mine you people are so much sharper
> if i wasn't so uneducated i would never have become a porter
> that woman's a bit stupid and she's even more uneducated
> than me almost crude in some respects
> POLLY: is she at all faithful to you?
> GALY GAY: yes because i've got the money

Then they give him chewing gum:

> GALY GAY: this is the first time for me but i think it tastes nasty
> POLLY: that's just at first once you've got its inmost taste on
> your lips you'll find your tongue can't do without this sport
> any more than a boxer his punchball

As he polishes off his gum Polly tells him 'your way of spitting out your gum is exactly like jip's except that it went to the left'. The riddle (p. 34) appears to follow, though it is even more idiotic than now, being concerned with how many peas go in a pot. Then comes Wang's entry (p. 30) to buy drink. 'I don't serve niggers or yellow men,' says Begbick as he orders 'seven bottles of good Old Tom Whisky for a white man'; and the scene ends with Uriah saying 'Jip won't be back now.'

[Scene: Bungalow/Late Afternoon]

The 1924/5 version therefore omits the reflections on 'personalities' (p. 31) and all the preliminaries to the elephant deal. However, they come into the outline sketch of a separate scene which follows the pagoda scene (our scene 7 above), in which *the three are packing their mg in grease galy gay is asleep on his chair*. This contains a first version of Uriah's speech about multiple opinions (p. 31), also an attack on 'personalities'; then when Galy Gay wakes up the soldiers pretend to be the voice of Buddha addressing him. Half awake, he knocks one of them flat and Blody 5 comes to see what the noise is about:

> URIAH: sorry sergeant we were just having a little game of golf

Bak (i.e. Polly) thereupon congratulates Galy Gay on his 'phenomenal right hook' and reckons that he would make mincemeat of a 'company of shiks' (i.e., presumably, Sikhs). He is applauded by 'eleven soldiers of the worchester regiment stationed at kilkoa', with whom he then drinks toasts to the Queen, the Regiment and others. Once they have left he tries to go as on p. 32 and the text continues much as now up to Polly's inquiry about the elephant on p. 34, after which the episode concludes with a few changes.

In the 1926 published script all these elements are brought together to make scene 8 virtually as we have it. Wang orders 'seven bottles of good old Victoria Whisky'; Uriah's order and his remark about 'taking beer on board' are not included, nor is Polly's second speech about the peculiar attractions of military life in wartime (p. 32). The passage from Galy Gay's 'But I fancy I'm the right man' (p. 34) to 'you can rob a bank', with its portrayal of him as a wrestler, is not included, so that Blody Five

appears almost at once after the riddle. Nor is Galy Gay's important remark about his wife's origin in a 'province where nearly
everyone is friendly', a phrase presumably added in the 1950s,
since it is not in the 1938 edition either. The 1926 scene ended
without the Alabama lines but with Blody Five reappearing to
shout 'The army's moving off to Tibet!' After which

> *Exit, whistling 'Johnny'. Galy Gay picks up his clothes and tries to
> sneak away quietly. The three catch him and fling him into a chair.*

The duplicated Arkadia script (1930 version) greatly economised
by eliminating the second and third pagoda scenes (our scenes 5
and 7) and rolling scenes 4, 6 and 8 into one single canteen scene.
It makes various cuts and changes: thus in scene 4 Blody 5 makes
a pass at Hiobja, while at its end Galy Gay is seated in a rocking
chair, denying that he carried Begbick's basket. Then Wang
enters to order drinks as in scene 8 and does his demonstration
with the drawing (our scene 5) in order to prove that his white
servant cannot be the missing man. The soldiers have decided
that they must get Galy Gay to go with them, when Blody re-
enters:

LEOKADJA: Cocktail or Ale?
BLODY: Ale!

When Blody says he needs a woman Begbick calls 'Hiobja!', and he
starts telling her about his pornographic pictures, much as in the
1924/5 version of scene 9. Begbick accuses him of abusing his
uniform, saying that he should wear rubber shoes and a dinner
jacket, after which the text is roughly as ours from Polly's 'But
how do we manage it . . . ?' (p. 30) to Galy Gay's 'I'm the right
man for any bit of business' (p. 34). Blody's reappearance and the
rest of the scene are approximately as in the 1926 version.

All this was altered in the 1931 production, where the latter
part of scene 4 was much changed, with Galy Gay falling asleep
after his denials and Begbick singing her verse offstage through
a megaphone. A version of scene 6 followed under the title of
Return of the three soldiers the same night, after which the half-curtain
was closed for Jip's verse monologue outside the pagoda (given
above). It reopened on a version of scene 8 taken largely from the
Arkadia script.

Interlude

This is not in the 1924/5 version. In the 1926 text it was to be spoken by Begbick 'alongside a portrait of Mr Bertolt Brecht'. This was replaced in the Arkadia script by a 'portrait of Galy Gay as a porter'. In 1931 the portrait remained but speech was shifted to make a prologue, being replaced by Jesse's long prose speech from pp. 41–2. In the 1938 Malik edition, as now, there was no mention of any portrait.

9. The canteen [10 in the 1926 version]

The 1926 text was very different from now, and a good deal longer. The setting to start with was '*canteen made of hollow bamboos and grass matting*,' which Leokadja and Hiobja are busy dismantling. Galy Gay arrives all agog as Uriah and Polly are wondering what form their business deal should take; asking Leokadja to lend them her elephant's head they develop their plot from that. Enter Blody 5 to show Hiobja his pictures:

> BLODY: hiobja i have a definite feeling that my sentiments for you have almost reached their peak scientifically speaking it's nothing for a girl to visit a man's room if he asks her only a swine would gossip about that my photographs are notable sights i have items you won't find in the british museum when you see them you may think them slightly too free but against that once you've seen them you never forget them
> HIOBJA: if they're truly scientific yes i'd like to see them but not in your room for a girl is a poor weak thing

Galy Gay takes a drink ('so that's gin it really does taste like a small fire') and the three soldiers assemble their elephant:

> KAKE: this tarpaulin makes so many folds in his belly that even leokadja begbick is blushing

Then Polly complains that he must work the tail by hand:

> KAKE: polly when you look out of the back it isn't decent
> URIAH: the front and back legs must be coordinated somehow or it'll look bad

Meanwhile Hiobja is showing Blody's pictures to the troops. There is a poker game with Leokadja, Hiobja and Blody, who announces:

> better for them to be tied with a triple rope and dumped in an anthill than to be drunk this a.m. when we move off not even a sergeant could expect mercy in such an eventuality

GALY GAY: that's order for you no matter whether it's a sergeant or an ordinary man he gets shoved in the hole

Among various disconnected snatches of dialogue here there is a Schweik-like reminiscence for Galy Gay:

> i had a friend a porter who in turn had a big red beard he could carry a hundredweight on his bare chest drank a pond dry daily and bashed the empire middleweight champion's eye flat for him this fellow had his beard removed one night because he'd seen a photo of the prince of wales and from then on he would run away from a chicken and couldn't lift more than 60 lb he was so scared of ghosts at night that he married a widow fancy that

Meantime Leokadja attacks Blody and tells him he would look better in civilian clothes. Then the artificial elephant is ready.

At this stage there appears to be no formal subdivision of the scene into separate 'numbers', nor is there an interspersed song. Galy Gay flings himself into the deal with 'One more swig' as in our text, while Uriah introduces Billy Humph as now. Galy Gay is by no means shocked at the latter's appearance:

> right billy you and i are going to get on splendidly as long as you're with me you can behave just like at home

Inside Billy, Bak (i.e. Polly) exclaims 'himmel arsch und wolkenbruch', prompting Galy Gay to ask 'did you say something billy'. Since Billy is 'a little souvenir of my grandfather' Galy Gay much regrets having to auction him:

> for instance i ride billy humph myself round the fortifications whenever i feel like it i may add i nurtured him at my bosom he was breastfed like you and me so everybody sing when he

comes up for auction since this is a moment i shall always
remember for after it's over my heart may well break
all sing 'it's a long way to tipperary' including billy

The auction follows, much as in our sub-scene II, though with
some additions, for instance:

SOLDIERS: billy what do you think of women?
BILLY *shits*
URIAH: that isn't nice of you billy you have a dirty mind

Galy Gay calls for bids, but is arrested. Blody Five enters in civilian
garb and Galy Gay chases the elephant out, shouting 'stop thief,
stop thief!'.

The next instalment, marked by Brecht *'blody's k.o.'*, corresponds
to our sub-scene IVa. Blody invites Hiobja to 'a few cocktails' and
reads the newspaper, making a hole in it to spy on the soldiers,
who are drinking cocktails too. Uriah pops the bowler hat on him
and asks 'where did you get this personality from, mister?'. But
Leokadja sings his praises:

eleven days after the battle of lake tchad river (mind how you
dismantle the bamboos up there) 50 blokes from the 42nd
who'd seen the devil face to face sneaked into a bungalow
drank paraffin and shot crazily at everyone who passed by
then a man arrived riding an elephant and addressed them
for five minutes on his own and decided they ought to be
shot after which 50 men came out and let themselves be mown
down in a heap like young sick lamas the name of this man
was blody five the batik man

They invite him to show his skill with a revolver, as on p. 55, but
using a cigar instead of an egg; then after he misses it the text
goes on (as also in 1926) with Blody cursing them as 'piss con-
tainers' and telling them how he won the name Blody Five by
shooting five 'Shiks' at the battle of 'Dschadseeluss', literally
Lake Chad River. In both versions the soldiers then comment on
his military virtues: 'and at the same time you're such a nice person. Kindly too, come to think of it'. In the 1924/5 text they then
have a sack race with him, after which he takes Hiobja on his
knee, is photographed by flashlight, and has to pay up.

The next sub-scene, marked by Brecht *'hongkong'*, has the three soldiers entering with Galy Gay and telling him that 'four hundred shiks, an entire battalion, are looking for you'. So they take the billiard table and use it as a boat in which to escape to Hongkong. They sing 'Nearer, my God, to Thee', as on the doomed *Titanic*, while Uriah cites a line from Brecht's early poem 'Tahiti' (which was also to be incorporated in a similar episode in *Mahagonny* scene 16). What looks like another version has Heep (i.e. Uriah) saying:

> raise your eyes jerome jip d'you see the widows on the shores of bombay see them waving their petticoats they're crying their eyes out and on sumatra your orphans will soon be oppressed by usurers

KAKE: it's just grey fields on the coastline and the wind whipping them   set the topsail there's going to be a storm tonight

BAK: hold tight jenny this gunboat is rocking dreadfully

KAKE: it's the atlantic rollers continually heaving up and down

GALGEI: hey you must go faster

HEEP: can you see a sail on the horizon behind us?

KAKE: no not yet

GALGIE: is it dangerous here   where have we got to?

KAKE: seven degrees east of ssw

BAK: if night doesn't fall too soon we can still make gibraltar

HEEP: the best thing would be to sing stormy the night to keep up our spirits have you any biscuits left?

KAKE: stormy the night is a fine thing when your spirits are getting low

GALY GAY [*sic*]: anyway let's just sing through it
they sing the seemannslos [asleep on the deep]

HEEP: now pipe down and best pray by yourselves for i think that's the island of tahiti the most charming island of them all where as many ships have gone aground as there are fish in the arctic sea

BAK: take off your hat you lout

HEEP: hear the wind whistling in the rigging?

GALY GAY: go quicker and go carefully for i tell you the wind's rising hour by hour

KAKE: yes and now we must strike the foresail who knows what will become of us if the storm goes on getting so much worse?

A '*flight to hongkong*' sub-scene follows, starting with a soldier asking the four 'Who are you?'

BAK: oh just tourists

SOLDIER: we know them and where's your luggage?

BAK: yes galgay where's the luggage?

URIAH: bak's got a straw hat

SOLDIER: which of you is galgay?

URIAH: oh nobody

SOLDIER: someone just mentioned the name galgay

URIAH: really did you hear that name?

SOLDIER: you know perfectly well it's the name of a notorious criminal

URIAH: anyhow my name isn't galgay and i wouldn't wish it to be

SOLDIER: is your name galgay?

GALGAY: me? certainly not

BAK: ah?

SOLDIER: did you say something?

BAK: not a word sir

SOLDIER: what's your name supposed to be sir?

GALGAY: jip jerome jip

SOLDIER: what are you?

GALGAY: porter sir

SOLDIER: what?

GALGAY: soldier i mean a thousand apologies

SOLDIER: no nonsense from you now that stolen elephant is written all over your face

KAKE: sir i object to your way of addressing our friend jerome jip i can answer for him personally

GALGAY: there you are

KAKE: indeed yes let us through this is our jip and these are my fists

SOLDIER: all right so long as you answer for him very well

BAK: that went off all right d'you want to look round hong-kong galgei?

GALGAY: kindly don't call me galgei they seem to know everything in this place and i don't want to look at hongkong but to hide

BAK: all right then wait on the pier a moment till we've gone

GALGAY: no no don't leave now it's terribly risky

URIAH: yes but we must get our paybooks stamped you'll have to wait here

GALGAY: i'll have to come along

BAK: out of the question it'd look as if you were scared just wait here a moment and keep an eye on my straw hat

GALGAY: where is it?

BAK: if you hold out you'll be allowed to see it   goodbye

SOLDIER: got your paybook on you?

GALGAY: yes here sir

an elephant appears at the back   galgay sees him

GALGAY: would you come over here sir i've got my paybook

SOLDIER: where are you off to   stay where you are

GALGAY: you can see my paybook very well over here sir

SOLDIER: you   what's that?

GALGAY: for god's sake what do you mean sir?

SOLDIER: don't tell me there's anything wrong with your eyesight just look where i'm pointing

GALGAY: an elephant

SOLDIER: emphatically an elephant very quick of you to spot it and who would you say that elephant belonged to eh?

Galy Gay wakes up and asks 'is this hongkong?', to be told by a soldier that it certainly isn't: it is Saipong. Then Blody Five appears and the episode ends with Galy Gay's protests as the soldiers threaten that he will be shot 'under the three ash trees of saipong'. 'oh uriah, ka, bak', he cries, 'help me!'

The *'trial'* sub-scene [numbered 5 by Brecht] corresponds to our III and is close to it as far as 'Yes, at Kankerdan I was with you' on p. 50, after which it goes on as in the 1926 version to where Galy Gay appeals to Uriah. Uriah then *'turns away'*, and as Galy Gay is marched off to be shot he sees Bak (ie. Polly) dressed as himself and exclaims 'there he is.'

GALY GAY: he was standing there all the time and i didn't see him

In the *'execution'* sub-scene they march Galy Gay off and on again to the sound of a drum, much as in the 1926 IV, which this resembles down to where Galy Gay is blindfolded. 'this galy gay in him has got to be shot', says Uriah. Bak bursts out laughing, but they shoot and he falls. Then Leokadja: 'what a noise you are making really you're pushing him too far now he really believes

he is dead he's just lying there but finish dismantling my walls
first it's two a.m.' In a fragmentary passage she goes on:

> without generals my sweet child you can make a war but
> without the widow begbick my dear boy you would just
> burst into tears as soon as things got hot and where there's a
> bar there'll be a urinal too that'll probably apply as long as
> the world lasts

SOLDIERS: widow begbick you can count on our acting accordingly
BEGBICK: ah yes it's a pleasant life i shan't be coming back here
  there are all kinds of places for widow begbick and as long as
  the army eats and drinks widow begbick won't grow old
  today was a fine day so tomorrow we'll be travelling north in
  those rumbling trains i've always been fond of cigars and
  words like afghanistan

The last sub-scene in the 1924/5 version is marked '6. *breaking
camp*'. As in the 1926 version it starts with the soldiers carrying in
the box – Begbick's piano apparently in this case – and singing
Chopin's Funeral March to the words 'Never again will the whisky
pass his lips' (twice). After Galy Gay has been told that he is to
deliver the funeral oration (p. 59) there are snatches of our present
text, followed by the greater part of the oration ('Therefore raise
up Widow Begbick's crate' etc. p. 63), then some dialogue where,
as in the 1926 version, the soldiers fit him out with equipment,
finishing up with the Anglo-German cry 'drei cheers für unsere
cäpten'. Elements of Galy Gay's verse speech (p. 60) are appended.
  In 1926 all this scene 9 material was pulled pretty well into its
present shape. The scene was divided into six music-hall 'numbers',
most of them followed by a verse of the Man equals Man song and
formally introduced by Uriah who blows a whistle and announces
the titles. Only IVa [5], the episode with Blody Five, is termed a
'subsidiary number'. The introductory section differs both from
the 1924/5 version and from our present text, but includes parts
of the latter, notably the concept of 'the man whose name must not
be mentioned'. Blody is not on till [2], the auction episode, though
his voice off is audible in [1] saying 'Johnny, pack your kit'; the
display of dirty photographs, much shortened, takes place in [5].
In [1], which is close to our version, Galy Gay is disturbed by the

elephant's ramshackle appearance, only cheering up in [2] when it becomes clear that Begbick will none the less buy it ('Elephant equals elephant, particularly when he is being bought'). After Galy Gay has been put in chains (p. 46) [2] continues with a dialogue between Leokadja and Blody, who desires her daughters but is at this point told to present himself in a dinner jacket and bowler hat. After that Blody's 'subsidiary number', deprived of the flashlight photo episode and all the passages of the 1924/5 version already cited, was shifted to follow the trial and execution, while the two Hongkong sub-scenes were cut.

[3], the Trial, is close to our text as far as 'at Kankerdan I was with you' (p. 50), but continues with Uriah's announcement of the verdict which is now in our IV (p. 51) as far as 'when a man is being slaughtered?' (p. 52), followed by a verse of the song. [4], the Execution, then follows on from there, starting with Begbick's next speech, and is virtually the same as our IV till Uriah's 'so that he can hear he's dead' on p. 54. This is where Blody enters in a dinner jacket and has his bowler hat rammed down by Uriah with the cry 'Stop your gob, civvy!'; verse 4 of the song follows. [5] then corresponds to our IVa, and starts with the dirty photographs, continuing with Uriah's 'Come on, Fairchild old boy!' (p. 55) and the shooting demonstration, done this time with eggs. The story about the five Shiks follows (cf. p. 56) leading straight into the Soldier's entrance as at the end of our version (p. 57). After this Blody wants to dance and calls for Hiobja, then makes do with her mother, saying 'Dame equals dame'.

[6], corresponding to our V, is announced by Uriah as on p. 57. The box this time is Begbick's nickelodeon; the Chopin march is sung as before; then comes an approximate version of our text as far as the long verse speech, with Begbick's speech about the move ('This army', p. 62) brought forward to where the trains now whistle (p. 60). The verse speech itself is shorter than now, but the rest of the sub-scene is much the same, with the addition at the end of the loading of the bundled-up Human Typhoon and the singing of the last verse of the song.

In the Arkadia script of 1930 there was no Man equals Man song, and the 'numbers' were announced by projections. Blody's entry in civilian clothes, seeking Hiobja, took place at the beginning of 1, which had the soldiers singing 'Widow Begbick's House in Mandalay' with the refrain 'Quick, Blody, hey' etc. He did not appear in 2, which ended with Galy Gay in chains and the singing of the Cannon Song. 3 was slightly shortened and 4 only began with the soldiers' complaints about the bad light (p. 53), then continued roughly as now to its ending. Next Blody appeared and the projector started showing the time, starting with 2 o'clock. There was no 'number' corresponding to our IVa. At 2.00 the soldiers decide to feed Galy Gay, and Begbick tells them to take the nickelodeon case and chalk his name on it, with a cross against it. At 2.01 he eats and the soldiers bring in the case, singing the Chopin march. At 2.03 Galy Gay starts practising his military movements (p. 59) and Begbick offers him castor oil. At 2.05 the trains start whistling and Begbick makes her speech about the move. Galy Gay washes as instructed by her (p. 62) and asks how many are going to Tibet (as in scene II of the 1926 version or our scene 10, p. 70) and so on to 'Women the same' (p. 70).

> GALY GAY: You know, Widow Begbick, one equals no one. So let me tell you there's not all that much difference between yes and no, and so I'm going to get rid of what I didn't like about myself, and be pleasant.

At 2.07 the waggons roll in with Begbick's Ale-Waggon hitched up to them, and the troops entrain. A projection says 'Funeral obsequies and graveside address for Galy Gay, last of the personalities, in the year 1928' and leads into the oration and the ensuing dialogue down to 'three cheers'. At 2.10 Polly delivers a harangue, ending up with an NCO-like 'one-two-three-four' repeated four times; then

> one-two-three . . .

> GALY GAY: Four! *Steps into the gap and marches radiantly behind the other three into the waggon, singing the Man equals Man song. The waggon rolls off.*

A projection then announces the title of our scene 11 and goes on: 'The shower capture it [i.e. the fortress] on behalf of Royal Shell. Private Jeraiah Jip is among them. You have seen how he can be used for any desired purpose. In our day he is used to make war.' A brief ending to the play follows.

For the 1931 production, Begbick's poem of the Flow of Things was included. The scene [9] began with a Voice as now; then the start followed, finishing with Galy Gay's 'I might have one for you' (p. 41) which led straight into 1. This was shortened, with a new bridge into 2, which added a new ending to the Arkadia version. 3 followed this version as far as Galy Gay's 'I think you're mistaking me' (p. 49), after which new material led into the next instalment of the song. In 4 there was a cut of about a page; in 4a of about a page and a half. 5 followed the Arkadia version as far as 'Women the same', then came 'Get entrained!' (p. 62) and the funeral oration, leading to the following ending of the play (which is also that of the 1938 Malik edition):

GALY GAY: Well, why haven't I got all my kit? (p. 63 bottom)
POLLY: A full set of uniform for our fourth man!
  The soldiers bring in the things and make a ring round Galy Gay so as to hide him from the audience. Meanwhile the band plays the war march and Begbick comes to the centre of the stage and speaks.
BEGBICK: The army is on the move to the northern frontier. The fire-belching cannon of the northern battlefields are waiting for them. The army is athirst to restore order in the populous cities of the north.
  The ring of soldiers opens. Galy Gay, Uriah, Jesse and Polly line up, with Galy Gay in the middle bristling with assorted weapons. They mark time to the music.
GALY GAY *loudly*: Who is the enemy?
URIAH *loudly*: Up to now we have not been told which country we are invading.
POLLY *loudly*: But it looks more and more like Tibet.
JESSE *loudly*: But we have been told that it is a pure war of defence.

Then Galy Gay speaks the concluding verses on p. 76, after which Begbick comes downstage and says 'Quod erat demonstrandum'. With the exception of this ending the Malik text of the scene is almost exactly the same as ours.

10. In the Moving Train [11 in 1926 version].

Like our scene 11 this was omitted from the Arkadia scripts, the 1931 production and the 1938 Malik edition, all of which ended with scene 9. In the 1950s Brecht restored it, using the 1926 text with small modifications of which the most significant was the insertion of the passage from 'Now you' to 'used to say' in Galy

Gay's speech on the Tibetan War (p. 66), with its indication that they are about to invade his wife's home.

The 1924/5 script contains two versions of the scene. In the first, which Brecht labelled '*old waggon scene*' the setting is as now, but it opens with the three developing a photograph (presumably that of Blody and Hiobja). The dialogue approximates to ours as far as Galy Gay's 'If this train doesn't stop' (p. 65) after which Blody wakes up, sees the three defaulters and tells them to arouse Galy Gay:

> he's got too good a conscience hey wake that man up i want to get a bit better acquainted with him man to man

He tells the three to hand over their revolvers, but is scared off when Uriah dons his (Blody's) bowler hat. Galy Gay then asks what has been going on, to which Kake (Jesse) replies:

> yesterday you got mixed up in some affair of a porter trying to sell an army elephant and being shot for it then you were taken ill and didn't want to be who you were
> GALY GAY: who was i then?
> KAKE: you're no better i see you were private jip but for quite a time you didn't know it and kept talking about a grass hut and a wife and stuff like that and you'd entirely forgotten all about being a soldier

They continue to confuse him about his identity, talking about his paybook and its description of him, the tattooing on his arms etc. Polly puts his head out of the window and is guillotined, then he does the same to Galy Gay and suggests that they all sing 'the bilbao men's song', whose text however is not given. The soldiers go off to play cards, and Galy Gay asks 'What is it that's shaking so?' (p. 64), after which the scene continues very roughly as now, but omitting the whole Fairchild episode and ending slightly differently, with the troops all singing 'Tipperary'.

The second version is headed '*2 Waggon-scene*' and is close to our text as far as Galy Gay's speech on the Tibetan War. Then Blody Five appears with a long monologue version of the self-castration episode (pp. 69–70), after which the rest is much as above.

[*Outside the Camp Signs of an Army on the Move*]

In this discarded scene from the 1924/5 script Jip appears to the tune of 'Tipperary' in search of the other three.

> BEGBICK: you're in luck they've announced a big theatre per-
> formance for this evening to fish people's money out of their
> pockets one of them is actually going to act an elephant calf
> which is a piece of pure malice on their part as he's already
> been brought to his senses once by the sale of a phoney ele-
> phant the man's called jerome jip you probably know him
> *jip hurries on*

When Blody appears, full of threats, Begbick roars with laughter and pushes her cart past him. Fragments then suggest that prior to the writing of the second waggon scene (above) this was to have been the self-castration scene. In one Blody delivers his monologue carrying '*a lamp a length of catgut and a breadknife*'; another gives a shorter version as follows:

> BLODY: there's nothing can be done to stop this sensuality
> which simply prevents you doing your duty the enemy is in
> your own house but the army which has so far earned noth-
> ing but glory cannot have its best men attacked by rot but
> even if there is no way of making your conduct sheet white
> once more at least a terrible example should be instituted
>
> since a strong unchastity originating in the womb
> hung my breadbasket ever higher and failed to
> respond to hard beds and unseasoned fare
> but often and repeatedly dragged me down among the animals
> i shall utterly etch away this excess and herewith
> shoot off my cock
> *goes into the undergrowth*

[*Theatre a Plank Stage beneath a Few Rubber Trees with Chairs Facing*]

This scene, only found in the 1924/5 script, is the performance subsequently detached to form the *Elephant Calf*. As far as the Sorrowing Mother's Speech (p 83) the text is almost word for word as now, except that it is Bobby Pall, not Jackie. Then Bak [Polly] says:

you may even be able to move them to tears it's the most moving bit if this goes over well perhaps i'll stay in the theatre for life *curtain rises* the elephant calf has had to leave because it feels unwell after those great proofs the criminal will be even deeper in the toils so tell me o elephant calf's mother something about thy son come deliver the sorrowing mother's speech

– which is differently worded. Then after the soldiers applaud and Uriah has told 'Jip' to 'Get on stage!' (p. 86):

galy gay trots along the footlights eyes the three and hums it's a long way as the soldiers cheer

URIAH: oh for christ sake drop that nonsense
BAK: he's waking up he's breaking through this damned notion of acting a singing elephant

Then Polly makes his speech (p. 86) asking if he thinks 'that this is thy mother?'

GALY GAY: it's a long way *cheers*
URIAH: you've misappropriated army funds
BAK: that's the disease you suffer from *aloud* the elephant calf has been overcome by the confusions of a guilty conscience
GALY GAY: get on with the play bak

The ending, after the Soldiers' 'It's a damned unfair business' (p. 86), is almost exactly as in our text except that the final song is omitted and two further pages are included after 'every decent human instinct' (p. 90). The closing stage direction adds *'to the singing of yes we have no bananas'*.

11. Deep in Remote Tibet Lies the Mountain Fortress of Sir El-Djowr [misnumbered 10 in the 1926 edition, which adds the direction *'Columns of troops are marching along singing the Man equals Man song'*.]

Like scene 10, this was omitted after the 1926 edition and re-introduced by Brecht in the 1950s. He then replaced the MG by a 'Kanone', cut Blody Five's entry (with his old catchphrase 'Johnny, pack your kit') and substituted Galy Gay's speech starting

'And I want to have first shot' (p. 72). After Galy Gay's call through the megaphone, too, the ending was different; the reference to the 'friendly people' from Sikkim once again dates from the 1950s. The verse comes from the conclusion of the Malik version of 1938, the final roll-call from that of 1926, which however ended with four marching off to the Man equals Man song and Polly calling back to the audience 'He'll be the death of us all yet'.

In the 1924/5 script there were several versions of this scene. One is virtually as in the 1926 edition. Another, called 'new last scene' is set in '*a dugout in tibet during an artillery bombardment*'. Enter the three soldiers asking if they can 'play a spot of pokker here?' [*sic*]. Blody, now quite subdued, is there and when Galy Gay enters they all stand up. He complains about the noise:

> if all this warfare doesn't stop soon i'm going to smash the place up *explosion* pokker demands total concentration above all how is one to bring off a decent royal flush with a din like this going on stop chewing your moustache sergeant

BLODY: i'm very sorry i'm afraid i forgot

In what seems the earliest version, marked by Elisabeth Hauptmann 'Summer 1925, Augsburg', the setting is '*canteen packing up towards morning signs of an impending move*', with Blody making all the troops except the machine-gunners do knees-bend. Jip arrives and is greeted, and a version of the first two-thirds of the present scene follows, as far as his exit (p. 74). Then there is a fragmentary '*long thin subdued conversation in the cool half-light*' between Galy Gay and Begbick, who thinks of selling her canteen and coming to Tibet with him. There is a long discussion with Hiobja, then Blody summons Galy Gay and the scene breaks off.

The version marked 'second ending' starts with Jip arriving as in the discarded 'outside the camp' scene above. The three enter, and Blody hobbles out of the undergrowth to introduce the real Jip, who is promptly knocked down by a hook to the chin from Galy Gay. Then comes '*Widow Begbick's canteen in the grey half-light. Noises outside of packing up and moving off.*' Confronting his friends much as on pp. 71–73, Jip curses them and is given Galy Gay's old paybook. Then Blody appears and marches the three off to the 'Johnny-wet-his-pants-wall', where they are shoved into an anthill.

Left alone with Begbick, Galy Gay orders 'a few cocktails and a cigar', and her approach to him (p. 74) follows. They are thinking of going to Tibet together as business partners; however, Blody summons him. Hiobja tells him she knows something discreditable about Blody, which makes Galy Gay slap Begbick's bottom and say they will get to Tibet all right. Blody then appears '*laughing horribly*' and asks Galy Gay who he is:

> GALY GAY: A man. Named Jeraiah Jip. And Man equals Man, my lad. But not a man equals not a man.

With that he gives Blody a stare, opens the window and asks the world what makes Lionel Fairchild, a sergeant in the Indian Army, speak so softly and prance like a stilt-walker.

> Suppose that in a rice-field near the Tibetan frontier, unobserved by other men but observed by a young girl, a man tears out his legendary sensuality by the roots with the aid of a penknife. Suppose he bellows like a donkey bellowing. Sergeant Blody Five, Human Typhoon, what's it like when you bellow?
>
> SOLDIERS *laugh louder*: Go on, Typhoon, bellow!
>
> BLODY FIVE *bellows*: Man equals Man. But Blody Five equals Blody – *his voice goes into a shrill falsetto* – Five.
>
> SOLDIERS *roaring with laughter*: He's chopped off his manhood! He's castrated himself!
>
> *Galy Gay bares his teeth in a smile and sits down. The laughter spreads backward until it is as though the whole Indian Army were laughing. Exit Blody Five, swept away by the laughter. A soldier in the window points at him.*
>
> SOLDIER: That was the Human Typhoon. And here – *indicating Galy Gay* – sits Jeraiah Jip who blasted him into Abraham's bosom as you might say. He'll be the death of us all yet. *Dance. Military music. It's a long way to Tipperary.*